W9-CII-086

CRUISIN' THE RIVER OF LIGHT

Devotions by Teens for Teens

SAINT LOUIS

Dedicated to the teen authors. They shine in God's river of light.

Then the angel showed me the river of the water of life, as clear as crystal, flowing from the throne of God and of the Lamb. ... The throne of God and of the Lamb will be in the city, and His servants will serve Him. They will see His face. ... There will be no more night. They will not need the light of a lamp or the light of the sun, for the Lord God will give them light. And they will reign for ever and ever.
Revelation 22:1–5

Unless otherwise noted, Scripture quotations are taken from THE HOLY BIBLE, NEW INTERNATIONAL VERSION®. Copyright © 1973, 1978, 1984 by the International Bible Society. Used by permission of Zondervan Publishing House. All rights reserved.

The "NIV" and "New International Version" trademarks are registered in the United States Patent and Trademark Office by the International Bible Society. Use of either trademark requires the permission of the International Bible Society.

Copyright © 1995 Concordia Publishing House
3558 S. Jefferson Avenue, St. Louis, MO 63118-3968
Manufactured in the United States of America

1 2 3 4 5 6 7 8 9 10   04 03 02 01 00 99 98 97 96 95

CONTENTS

INTRODUCTION

Where are you on the river?

River—a metaphor for life. Along the river—all the sights and sounds of life. Good times and calm waters. Struggles, through the rapids. Challenges, past toxic waste and uncharted waters. Places along the river where you shouldn't venture. Places to stop, take a dip, and have a great time.

Life is like a river. So is our faith life. Some days being a Christian is pretty smooth sailing. Other days, there are rapids all over. What a blessing to have God as our navigator for whatever life's waters may hold.

The devotions in this book reflect the thoughts of teens traveling on the river. They reflect the hope and confidence God gives His people as they confront life's challenges. They're not out to convince us that travel on the river is ever easy. But they do help us see that the trip can be made safely when God is at the helm, guiding our journey.

Join these young authors on the river. They have some neat insights and a wonderful faith in Christ to share!

Terry Dittmer
The Board for Youth Services
St. Louis

Rebecca Wiechman

GOD DID IT!

Bible Reading: Genesis 1–3

The biology teacher stood in front of the class and pointed at a chart. At one end of the chart was an ape with long swinging arms, and at the other end, a hairy kind of stooped-over man. The teacher smiled and said, "This is how man evolved."

One boy, a little confused and fearful, shot his hand in the air and said, "But I believe in the Bible." The class waited silently, but the teacher quickly dismissed the comment and continued, "This is how we …"

The boy raised his hand, more timidly this time, and said quietly, "God made Adam, the first man, right?" The teacher paid no attention at all.

This situation occurs many times in schools across the country. How do we reconcile what we read in Genesis with what we hear in science class? How do Adam and Eve fit with an anthropologist's idea of the "first man"?

The world constantly tries to say the story of creation is made up. But as Christians we remember *God did it!* We are definitely not here by accident, nor are we here to merely please ourselves during our short stay on earth. We owe our existence to God. Every atom of hydrogen, every star in the sky, and every blade of grass is here because God wants it to be. In Genesis, God, the artist,

7

signs His picture saying, "This is Mine."

God pays us a high compliment in Genesis. After making everything else, God made man. In fact, He made man in His own image, holy and blameless. When He was finished with all of creation, God commented to Himself, "Very good." He even put Adam in charge of His creation. He was obviously satisfied, and no one except God has ever been completely satisfied with man since then!

We were made good and perfect, but temptation and sin lurked just around the corner. We have lived with the consequences of sin ever since, but, thankfully, we don't have to live with the punishment. God promised Adam and Eve, and us, forgiveness and salvation in His own Son.

The next time you learn about evolution, just remember "God did it!" State your case, and if the teacher disagrees, just remember—you are not the descendant of an ape but rather of a perfect God.

Prayer: Lord, help me through the times my faith in You is put to the test. Help me remember You did it—You created the whole universe. Give me the courage to share this fact with people who don't know it. In Jesus' name. Amen.

FIGHT THE GOOD FIGHT

Bible Reading: 2 Timothy 4:7

"Do you guys mind if I get up and go to church tomorrow?"

That was all it took to send Melissa into gales of laughter. Everyone at our table looked at her as she announced, "Janelle's going to church tomorrow!" The table exploded with laughter and I was close to tears. One girl asked if I went to the Church of the Black Savior, a church for Satan worshipers.

I ran to my room in tears. I hadn't cried since the night before I left for Dartmouth. I was a junior in high school, going to a debate workshop at the New Hampshire college. My parents had prayed with me that night when I was so nervous about leaving home for the first time. I remember thinking the prayer was pretty stupid. What was God going to do, stand beside me and hold my hand? Now I realized how important those prayers really were.

That week my roommates had bugged me every night when I read my devotions. On Friday night I read a devotion called "Steer Your Peers." I knew my time to stand up as a Christian had come. But trying it in the cafeteria the next morning had left me confused and hurt, unable to understand why my friends would persecute me for believing in Jesus.

I called my parents and they offered advice and prayers. I wasn't sure then which I needed more. Sunday morning I went quietly to church. Everyone there was so kind that I almost cried again. These strangers were more my friends than my campus-mates because we shared a common Lord.

A few days later I received two letters from friends at home saying they had prayed for me that Sunday. My youth pastor sent me a card and wrote on it, "I have fought the good fight, I have finished the race, I have kept the faith" (2 Timothy 4:7).

I came home from Dartmouth a different person. I know now that nothing's too tough for me and God, armed with His Word and a lot of prayers. I'm not afraid to speak up for Christ anymore.

Go ahead. Take a stand. Fight the fight with Jesus at your side.

Prayer: Father in heaven, give me the courage to stand up for Christ. Remind me that You hold me in the palm of Your hand and will help me in every situation. Amen.

HE GATHERS THEM IN HIS ARMS

Bible Reading: Isaiah 40:11

Alissa's face was white and she trembled as she came up to me. "Can I talk to you?" she whispered. Concerned, I put Darrel in charge of picking up the puzzles and took Alissa to a quiet corner. I had been helping after school at my church's day-care center for two months. This was the first time Alissa had ever spoken to me at all.

"What is it, sweetheart?" I asked. Her face crumbled. "I'm scared," she sobbed. The story came out in gasping hiccups, and I cried too. A man in Alissa's apartment building had lured her into his apartment to see his new kitten. Then he had sexually abused her. There was no way to tell how long the abuse had been going on. He had told Alissa that he would kill her mommy and daddy if she told on him. But he hadn't said he would kill me.

I hugged Alissa and promised her that the man would not hurt her again. I left her with one of the adult helpers and ran to find the center's director and Pastor Youngman. We called Alissa's parents and the police.

The police found the man's apartment filled with pornographic pictures of children. Alissa's parents began the painful process of legal proceedings and found counseling for Alissa and themselves. It was many weeks before light came into Alissa's eyes, which had been vacant and filled with pain ever since I first saw her.

I was haunted by the evil of the man who had abused Alissa. And I blamed myself for not knowing something was wrong. Five-year-old children don't sit quietly doing nothing for hours at a time. Why hadn't I worked harder with Alissa, talked to her, gotten her to talk to me earlier? Confused and depressed, I asked Pastor Youngman if I could talk to him.

"Megan, you did nothing wrong in this situation," he said. "You saved Alissa from suffering longer. You think you did nothing—but why did she come to you? Why not to me or Mrs. Allan? You had reached her, Megan, in some way you didn't realize. She trusted you enough to share her frightening secret."

I cried and Pastor held my hand. We prayed together. Prayed for forgiveness and miraculous change for the man who had abused Alissa. Prayed for Alissa that she could feel whole and clean and safe in Jesus' arms. Prayed for Alissa's parents that they could feel peace after the horror of what happened, and that they could share that peace with Alissa.

"Jesus is your Shepherd, Megan," Pastor Youngman said as I left. "He holds you and Alissa safe in His arms."

Prayer: Jesus, keep all the Alissas of the world safe in Your arms. Protect them from the horror of abuse and neglect. Use me to reach out to Your lambs and comfort them with Your love. Amen.

FRIENDS

Bible Reading: Proverbs 18:24

Margaret and I have been best friends since the first day of first grade. Growing up, we were inseparable. I can't see her picture or say her name without recalling some silly stunt we pulled, like the time I accidentally gave her a black eye! Now we live a thousand miles apart, but we still burst into laughter over nothing when we talk. The phone company could use us for a commercial. Margaret seems to know my thoughts better than I do. We've always been there for each other, no matter how many miles separated us.

The closeness Margaret and I share is no accident. We developed our trust and friendship over a long period of time. I thank God that He gave me a friend to share in joyful times and in troubled times. Maybe you have a friend like Margaret, whose smile makes you laugh and whose shoulder is there for you to lean on.

God talks about close friends when He says, "There is a friend who sticks closer than a brother" (Proverbs 18:24). Just how close is "close"? According to Jesus, the ultimate demonstration of love for a friend is the laying down of your own life. We might have to think twice about giving our lives for a friend. Jesus didn't. He gave His life, not only for those who cared for Him, but for those who made fun of Him and rejected Him too.

Jesus' example models friendship for us. He shows us how to love at all times—not just when we're in the mood or a friend is treating us right. He shows us how to love when our best friend makes team captain and we don't. Friendship centered in Christ rises above everyday problems and soars to heights of understanding and love.

Friendship can be a risk. When you become friends with people, you give a piece of your life to them, and they to you. You develop a lifetime of memories—some that are pleasant, and perhaps some that you'd just as soon forget. Jesus gave much more than a piece of His life. He lovingly gave up His whole life to win you forgiveness and salvation.

The next time you are with a close friend, before you start laughing and joking around, tell that friend that you thank God for your close friendship. Go ahead. Take the risk.

Prayer: Lord, thank You for placing good friends in my life. Forgive me when I take them for granted and forget to let them know what they mean to me. Thank You for being my best friend and for giving Your life for me. Amen.

WORRIES

Bible Reading: Matthew 6:25–34

MONDAY!!!

How many times have you gotten up on that first day of the school week with that groan on your lips? I can't count how many times I have. There's the homework you put off until Saturday, and then Sunday, and now it's still not done. There's the big math test staring you in the face. You know—the one you didn't study for. And if that isn't enough, Mom's yelling at you to get out of bed—you're already 10 minutes late for the bus!

And then you finally get to school, cramming your brains out, and settle into class. Math. A huge test. And then it happens. Total mind-blank. You read the first question. It seems that there is no possible answer. You can't remember one single formula or equation.

After muddling your way through the hardest test you've ever taken, you head to your second class. Choir. Usually a pretty straightforward class—you come, you sing, you leave. But not today. Today the director asks you to sing the hardest solo in the school musical, the one you haven't looked at in a month.

So after embarrassing yourself in front of 80 classmates, you to go third period. History. "Guess what!" says the teacher. "Pop quiz!" And then you go to fourth period …

Well, you get the picture. Ever had one of those days? Yeah, so have I. But Jesus has good news for us, even on those kinds of days. He says, "Look at the birds of the air; they do not sow or reap or store away in barns, and yet your heavenly Father feeds them. Are you not much more valuable than they? Who of you by worrying can add a single hour to his life?" (Matthew 6:26–27).

You don't see birds worrying about school, home-work, chores, practices, little brothers and sisters. ... But how on earth can we handle all those things without worrying? Jesus gives us that answer a few verses later. "Seek first His kingdom and His righteousness, and all these things will be given to you as well" (Matthew 6:33). Jesus has won a place for us in His righteous kingdom. He loved us enough to give His life for us. He gives us new life in Him, helping us take on every trouble that comes our way.

Instead of worrying about that math test, pray about it! God will give you His guidance. But don't think God wants you to slack off. God will help you get a good grade by helping you study. And He'll give you a lot more help as you study His Word. Then, "That math test is going to be so-o-o-o-o-o-o hard! I just know I'm going to flunk" is replaced by "That math test is pretty tough, but with God's help and a little elbow grease, I ought to ace it!"

Try this. Look at last week on the calendar and remember all the things you worried about. Now look ahead to what's happening this week. Lay all your worries at God's feet. He will lift that giant lead weight off your shoulders. He'll help you get up in the morning, go to school, get to practice and work, and even breathe a little easier through it all. At the end of the week, look back and see the difference. There will be a difference. God guarantees it.

Prayer: Father, Son, and Holy Spirit, ease my worries by helping me focus my life on You and Your Word. In Jesus' name I pray. Amen.

A Promise to Stand On

Bible Reading: Romans 8:28

Erin wheeled her wheelchair to the side of the pew. Though she was surrounded by family and friends that Easter Sunday, she looked bitter and alone. Erin was disabled. An accident three years before had left her paralyzed from the waist down.

Erin was a straight-A student and had been an outstanding basketball player. The accident destroyed Erin's dream of winning a scholarship to play on a college team. Erin was devastated. She blamed God for what had happened to her.

But that Easter morning, Erin noticed a little girl across the aisle a few rows down. She too was in a wheelchair. Erin watched her the entire sermon. The bitter expression on the little girl's face matched the one she had worn for so long.

The pastor read a verse that Erin hadn't thought about in a long time, "In all things God works for the good of those who love Him, who have been called according to His purpose" (Romans 8:28). Erin began to examine her attitude during the past years and realized she didn't like it. Surely God hadn't caused her to have the accident. But could God bring some good from her paralyzed body? Could it be that He wanted her to be a friend to this little girl and help her deal with her disability?

You may not be paralyzed, but you've probably blamed something on God and then later realized, through the Holy Spirit's prodding, that He is in control after all. James 1:2 says, "Consider it pure joy, my brothers, whenever you face trials of many kinds, because you know that the testing of your faith develops perseverance."

Our Father is an all-knowing, all-giving, all-caring God. He loves us so much that He gave His Son to die on the cross for our sins. A God who loves us this much does not leave us in despair, but works through every trouble and temptation for our good. Sometimes we might be able to see the good God is accomplishing through our pain, sometimes we might have to wait until heaven to understand. But always we will know that His Holy Spirit is making our faith stronger.

How awesome it is to have a God who knows what we are going through and loves us, even when we falsely blame Him for the things that go wrong instead of praising Him. He will never leave us. That's a promise to stand on.

Prayer: God, when I am disabled by sin, hurt feelings, and other kinds of pain, let me trust in Your loving and good will for me. In Jesus' name. Amen.

MARRIED? ME?

Bible Reading: Proverbs 31:10

An old Arabic legend tells about a powerful sultan who had many wives. Of all his wives, he treasured Lark the most. She was graceful, with a quiet charm. He constantly feared that Lark would no longer love him, for she was very young and he was past middle age.

To test her love, the sultan had his jeweler design a unique ring for his young wife. He knew that if she were to commit adultery, she would have to remove the ring. So he did not tell her the secret of the ring—it was designed to fall apart if removed from her finger. He feared for the day that she would come to him with the ring in pieces, for he knew that would be the day that he would have to order her execution. The ancient laws of Arabia were strict—to betray the sultan meant instant death, even for a favored wife.

The sultan called his wife to him and gave her the ring. He explained that the four bands of the ring represented the four seasons. She would be his true love for each season as they passed, one after another. The interwoven design was a symbol of their lives, one pouring into the other, each depending on the other to create the whole. Lark was so pleased with her husband's gift that she fell more deeply in love with husband than ever. She never removed the ring from her finger.

As a senior in high school, I often find myself thinking of whom I might marry. Proverbs 31:10 says "A wife of noble character who can find? She is worth far more than rubies." That can be said for a husband too. Finding a trustworthy spouse is difficult in the best of times, let alone in the immoral times we live in now.

The story of the sultan and Lark is one of true love. I hope God will bless me so. Marriage can be a risky business. But marriage in which both husband and wife turn to Christ for forgiveness and leadership is marriage built on a strong foundation.

Prayer: Father, give me the wisdom of Solomon and the love of Christ in my own life. Lead me to a spouse with whom I can grow, and who I myself can nurture in Your love. In Jesus' name. Amen.

TRAVELS WITH MY GRANDMOTHER

Bible Reading: John 11:25–26

Grandmother died on a Friday evening. Mom and Dad had left for Green Bay, Wisconsin, Friday afternoon, knowing she would not live much longer. They didn't make it in time. Sunday morning we prayed for my family in church.

After the service, Mrs. Terrence asked if my brother and I were going to the funeral Monday morning. All I said was no, but Mrs. Terrence probably realized that our family just didn't have the money for all of us to make the trip. We talked a little bit about Grandmother. She had always been a Christian model for our family. Dad said she was responsible for his decision to become a pastor. Grandmother had been thrilled when Jared said he was going to go to the seminary, and she loved hearing about my youth group events.

Jared and I stopped at McDonald's on the way home from church.

The phone was ringing when we got home. I picked it up and Mrs. Terrence said, "Chad, there are two tickets to Milwaukee waiting for you at the Los Angeles airport. We'll call the high school in the morning and get you and Jared excused from classes."

My mouth was still hanging open when Mr. Nichols,

another friend of Mom and Dad's, pulled up in front of the house. He handed Jared and me an envelope with $200 in it. "For a bus ride to Green Bay," he said.

Jared and I had one hour to pack and get to the airport. If we'd had time to think about it, we'd probably never have accepted so generous a gift. Driving across Wisconsin that night, it was as if Grandmother traveled with us. We talked about how we, as little boys, tried to be the first to spy her getting off the plane when she came to spend Christmas with us. How she wanted to attend every single Christmas service that was scheduled to hear Dad preach and hear us sing. How she'd wait till Mom and Dad left the room, and then sneak over to shake packages under the tree and guess what was inside.

Talking with Grandmother had always been like talking to someone my own age. She seemed to always understand exactly how I was feeling, and she never put me down. She made me feel like a million dollars for every little accomplishment, from getting my first job to making the varsity squad.

"Grandmother was like Jesus to us," I told Jared that night. "She always loved us, no matter what."

"That's right," he agreed. "Now she lives with Him."

Prayer: Father, thank You for the people in my life who are Jesus to me. The people who tell me about the salvation and forgiveness He won for me. The people who accept me, unconditionally, as He does. In Jesus' name. Amen.

By Faith, Not by Sight

Bible Reading: 2 Corinthians 4:15; 5:7

It was electrifying news—Jesus Christ had risen from the dead, just as He had said He would! "We have seen the Lord!" some of the disciples cried. But Thomas couldn't bring himself to believe it. "Unless I see the nail marks in His hands and put my finger where the nails were, and put my hand into His side, I will not believe it" (John 20:25).

Thomas' doubt evaporated a week later when he saw the resurrected Christ face-to-face and examined His wounds. Then Jesus told him, "Because you have seen Me, you have believed; blessed are those who have not seen and yet have believed" (John 20:29).

"Those who have not seen and yet have believed." That describes you and me. We have been called to worship the invisible God. Our faith does not rest on physical signs or manifestations. Our beliefs sometimes go contrary to what logic and physical sense indicate. Faith is "being sure of what we hope for and certain of what we do not see" (Hebrews 11:1).

"So," Paul wrote, "we fix our eyes not on what is seen, but on what is unseen. For what is seen is temporary, but what is unseen is eternal. ...We live by faith, not by sight" (2 Corinthians 4:18; 5:7).

I have no idea what the future holds in store for me or for you. We walk through life trusting in Jesus our Shepherd to lead us safely. Our path at times will wind through green pastures and beside still waters. At other times it may traverse the valley of the shadow of death. But God is with us today as He was with His people long ago.

As Christians, we have the advantage of knowing that the steps we take in faith lead to a definite and positive goal. Peter explains this comforting truth when he writes, "Though you have not seen Him, you love Him; and even though you do not see Him now, you believe in Him and are filled with an inexpressible and glorious joy, for you are receiving the goal of your faith, the salvation of your souls" (1 Peter 1:8–9).

Prayer: Father, I can't see You, but I know with certainty that You are with me and that You loved me enough to send Your only Son to the cross for me. Give me Your Holy Spirit's help to cling to that certainty always. Amen.

It's by My Spirit

Bible Reading: Zechariah 4:6

My little brother John was born with Down's Syndrome. My family had a difficult time adjusting to that fact right after he was born. How would John get along when he wouldn't be able to do all the things that other kids his age could do?

One night we read a verse from the Old Testament. "This is the word of the LORD ... 'Not by might nor by power, but by My Spirit, says the LORD Almighty' " (Zechariah 4:6). In a vision, God told His prophet Zechariah to depend not on might or power, but on His Holy Spirit.

John will never have all the "might and power" that other kids his age have. But that's okay. Nothing we have in life depends on our own might and power. We're proud of John for his own efforts. And, more importantly, we know Jesus loves him.

God shows us over and over in His Word that our own power and might accomplishes little. Gideon thought he needed a huge army to defeat the Midianites. But God sent men away until there were only 300 soldiers in Gideon's army. That victory was the Lord's, won with His might and power. Joshua too knew who would win the battle of Jericho when he marched his people around the city seven times and then commanded, "Shout! For the LORD has given you the city!" (Joshua 6:16).

It is tempting to accept all the praise for ourselves when we feel we have accomplished something great. In those times, along with feeling good about what we have accomplished, we thank God for the power and might His Holy Spirit put in us at our Baptism. It is God's power in us that helps us accomplish things and, best of all, helps us believe in Jesus' victory on the cross.

Prayer: Jesus, remind me that I don't have to accomplish everything with my own talent and strength. Fill me with Your power and might that I might, in Your grace, accomplish all You set before me. Amen.

FORGIVE, AGAIN AND AGAIN

Bible Reading: Matthew 18:21–22

Jordan dashed home from first grade, thrust the door open, dropped his book bag on the floor, and yelled, "Mommm-y!"

"What, honey? I'm in the kitchen. Come here."

Jordan raced into the kitchen, "Boy, those cookies smell great, Mom."

Mom looked up and gasped, "Jordan! What happened to your eye?"

Jordan stared at his shoes. "Jake punched me and gave me a black eye." Tears poured down his cheeks.

"Why would Jake do that to you? I thought he was your best friend."

"I said I didn't want to play with him at recess," Jordan explained.

"That's no reason to punch you! I'm going to call Jake's parents."

"Yeah, Mom. And tell them to nail Jake. I'm so mad I'd like to …"

"Wait, Jordan," Mom interrupted him, putting a hand on his shoulder. "I'm not setting a good example for you at all. Jake was wrong to punch you. And you should not let people hurt you. But we need to sit down with him and talk this out."

Jordan's mom remembered the many times God instructs us to forgive one another in His Word. In Matthew 6:14–15, Jesus says, "If you forgive men when they sin against you, your heavenly Father will also forgive you. But if you do not forgive men their sins, your Father will not forgive your sins." That's a tough statement, and impossible for us to do without God's example and the help of His Holy Spirit. Paul tells us, "Be kind and compassionate to one another, forgiving each other, just as in Christ God forgave you" (Ephesians 4:32).

It's tempting when friends hurt us to hold a grudge and long to hurt them back. Like Jordan's mom we remember God's plan for relationships, "Bear with each other and forgive whatever grievances you may have against one another. Forgive as the Lord forgave you" (Colossians 3:13).

Prayer: Jesus, when I'm tempted to hurt people as badly as they hurt me, remind me of the way You forgave Your enemies, even as You suffered at their hands. Help me share Your forgiveness with others. Amen.

CELEBRATE LIFE

Bible Reading: Psalm 139

Nobody likes me. I'm not pretty enough or smart enough or clever enough. I'm never going to school again.

Have you ever felt that way? I have—a lot lately. What do I do? How do I get up in the morning? I remember some of the things that have happened in my life and what God taught me through them.

I was only three weeks old when God saved me from death. I was born with a cleft palate—an opening in the roof of my mouth. The young interns who examined me at birth didn't even notice it. The cleft palate caused feeding problems and made me lose so much weight that my parents rushed me to the hospital on Christmas Day. Those same two doctors were in the emergency room, fighting to save my life.

God has a plan for each of us, even as we grow in our mother's womb (Psalm 139:13–16). God used those doctors that day to keep His purpose for me alive.

Last year I had major surgery on my back. God taught me a lot as I lay in the hospital. The nurses understood what I was going through and helped me through the rough times. My classmates and friends and family kept me in their prayers. Through their cards and phone calls and visits they reminded me that I was in their thoughts and that God was still in control of my life. If I can live through a five-hour surgery and be back on my feet in less than a week, God can help me face anything with His courage and strength.

You are special. God had a plan for you before you were even born. Paul tells us, "For while we are in this tent [earthly body], we groan and are burdened, because we do not wish to be unclothed but to be clothed with our heavenly dwelling, so that what is mortal may be swallowed up by life. Now it is God who has made us for this very purpose and has given us the Spirit as a deposit, guaranteeing what is to come" (2 Corinthians 5:4–5). God works in you through His Word, your Baptism, and His Supper He gave you to keep the saving work Jesus did on the cross at the center of your life. No matter what happens or how you feel, God's Holy Spirit is working in you to complete His plan and to give you a perfect home in heaven.

Have you ever felt like no one loves you? Read John 3:16. God loved you enough to send His Son to die for you. Have you ever felt like you aren't pretty enough or smart enough or clever enough to keep up with your classmates? You aren't like anyone else. God made you special and different. And, through the saving work of His Son, He makes you perfect.

> **Prayer:** God, help me celebrate the plan You have for my life. When I put myself down, lift me up through the loving arms of Your Son. In His name. Amen.

Lost Lambs

Bible Reading: Luke 15:3–7

Blake's face was white under his tan. "Two of the kids are missing," he said. "Kayla and Melissa."

I looked at the line of 50 children, marching behind our church's Christian flag, up the cliff to the bus. "Stay here and get the kids on the bus," I told Blake. "I'll tell Pastor Mike and go look for them." I ran to tell our youth pastor that Kayla and Melissa hadn't lined up with their counselor. He talked to the lifeguard in the area where we'd been sitting and together they began to look for the girls. I ran down the beach, praying that I would find the little girls playing safely in the sand.

Up until now my job as assistant day-camp director with Pastor Mike had been relatively uneventful. I had spent the afternoon rubbing sunblock on sandy little bodies and helping kids build sand castles. Every half hour I blew a whistle, and 50 kids ran from every direction to line up behind their counselors by the Christian flag we'd used to stake out our spot at the beach. After counting noses the last time, I'd told them they could play for 30 more minutes, then we'd clean up to go home.

I'd blown the clean-up whistle and soon our line of little soldiers was marching back to the bus—except for Kayla and Melissa. "Please, God," I prayed. "Please let them be all right." I ran along the water line. Surely they hadn't been swept out into the ocean with a wave. They knew they weren't allowed to go in the water without Blake right beside them.

Before long I had raced almost two miles up the beach, stopping at each lifeguard station I passed. Finally, ready to dissolve into tears, I heard little voices shrieking my name. "Mandy, we're over here!" I looked to the closest lifeguard station. There they were, jumping up and down by the lifeguard who was talking into his radio phone, telling Pastor Mike the lost had been found.

I threw my arms around the girls and cried for joy. They had turned the wrong direction when they came out of the bathroom. Instead of asking for help, they had walked along the beach, looking for our Christian flag.

We walked back to a busload of cheering kids and counselors. Then and there Pastor Mike announced a new rule about only going to a restroom with a counselor along. Then he told the kids the parable of The Lost Sheep. "Kayla and Melissa were our lost lambs," he said. "Now the angels in heaven are having a party because Kayla and Melissa are safe. And that's what the angels do when we tell God we're sorry, after our sins have led us away from Him. Let's go back to church and have a party!"

Prayer: Jesus, my Good Shepherd, when sin and worry and fear take me away from You, bring me gently back to Your arms. Forgive my sins and let me rejoice with Your angels. Amen.

Rachael Waser, Andy Vangilder, Chip Hallsten, Robyn Gerber

DRINKING, IS IT WORTH IT?

Bible Reading: Proverbs 20:1

I'm so bored, Mary Ann thought to herself. Why did she have to baby-sit on New Year's Eve? Why couldn't she be out with Todd, having the time of her life? She flipped around the TV channels. It was 11:30 and nothing was on.

Then the doorbell rang. Who could that be? "Todd, Derek!" she exclaimed as she opened the door.

"We thought we'd stop by and see our favorite baby-sitter," Todd grinned. That made Mary Ann smile. He could always make her smile.

"You can't stay for long," Mary Ann said, pretending not to notice the 12-pack Derek was carrying. She went to the kitchen to get something to eat and returned to the living room to find Todd and Derek drinking beer. She started to tell them to stop, but then thought about how much it would impress Todd if she joined in. So she took a sip now and then, acting as if she were having a great time.

The next thing Mary Ann knew, Derek was throwing up! It smelled awful. Todd was just about asleep. Mary Ann panicked. The parents would be home anytime. The house reeked. Finally Derek stopped throwing up. Together, they walked Todd to the car and shoved him in the backseat. Derek took off, swerving down the road.

Mary Ann cleaned up the house as well as she could.

When the children's parents came home, she told them she had been sick. The next morning she heard the news. Derek had swerved into an oncoming truck. Both boys were in critical condition.

Alcohol touches all of us in some way. It destroys life, health, and reputations. You may be tempted to drink yourself—just for one night of fun, or you may be worried about a friend or family member who is drinking. God doesn't fool around when it comes to drinking. In Proverbs He says, "Wine is a mocker and beer a brawler; whoever is led astray by them is not wise" (Proverbs 20:1).

Jesus cared enough about people at a wedding celebration to make more wine for them to drink. But He also cares so much about you that He gave His life for you. He will be right beside you when you are tempted to drink, or to drive with someone who has been drinking, helping you make decisions about the life that is precious to Him.

Prayer: God, thank You for the many gifts You have given me—my body, my mind, and the ability to make decisions to Your glory. Be with me when I'm tempted to use and abuse alcohol. Guide me in helping the people I love to make wise choices. In Jesus' name. Amen.

Phil Palacios, Laurie Schultz, Krista Evans,
Brian Schwartzmeyer

SECOND CHANCE

Bible Reading: Isaiah 41:10

Debbie's mom reached over the railing of the hospital bed and held her hand. "Why?" she asked. Debbie sighed and sat up straight in the bed. She started telling the story that led to her attempted suicide.

Debbie. Pretty. Popular. Good grades. Captain of the volleyball team. Why would she try and take her own life?

A series of events led Debbie into depression. Her favorite grandmother died in November. A teacher misgraded her science test, gave her a low grade, and refused to admit her mistake. Rushing to class on a rainy day, Debbie slipped and broke her ankle. Volleyball was out of the question.

Even tougher problems were building up at home. Dad came home late often, complaining about "business problems" that had to be fixed. Debbie sensed the tension building between her parents. One night Dad came home even later than usual, his clothes mussed and his hair a mess, and Mom screamed that she knew he was having an affair and she was going to file for a divorce.

When Debbie's boyfriend broke up with her before the Valentine's dance, she felt completely alone. She couldn't talk to her parents—maybe if she gave them no trouble at all it would somehow help to save their marriage. Ben, her brother, was as upset as she was. Talking to him tended to lead to arguments, and that would upset their parents even more.

Debbie became withdrawn. She rarely went anywhere with her friends. Her grades plummeted and she cut classes. Some mornings it seemed impossible to get out of bed. When she managed to finish a story or poem for English class, it was about death. She commented to her friend Carrie that she wished she could die and be with her grandmother.

Debbie's depression deepened. One afternoon she took a butcher knife to her room and slit her wrists. Ben found her and called 911.

"And that's that," Debbie finished.

"But, honey, why didn't you tell me how you felt?" Mom asked.

"I didn't want to bother you," Debbie said. "And I didn't think anybody else would care."

"Debbie, I do care, and so do Dad and Ben and your friends. I've talked to the doctors. We're going to get you the help you need to get through this."

Tears ran down Debbie's cheeks. "I thought everyone had given up on me, even God," she said.

Mom reached over the bed to hug Debbie. "God will never give up on you, even when you think you've reached your limit. God promises that He will never let you be tempted beyond what you can handle. He's holding you in His hands right now, and He'll give us all the strength we need to get you well."

Debbie smiled through her tears and hugged her mom back. "I guess I need to thank God for giving me another chance at life."

Prayer: God, depression scares me. Lead me to people who can help me when I feel down. Help me listen to my friends and hear their cries for help. Remind me every day that I am Your chosen and valuable child, made precious by the sacrifice of Your Son. In His name. Amen.

A SPIRITUAL BONFIRE

Bible Reading: John 1:9

A bonfire—how neat! Our youth group had decided to have a bonfire in the woods behind our pastor's house.

We gathered Sunday night and watched Mike, our youth leader, start the fire. He lit some newspaper and, before long, the logs were crackling. The circle of kids around the fire grew bigger and bigger.

When the embers were red and glowing, Vicki, our pastor's daughter, and I went to the house to get the hot dogs. It was cold and dark away from the fire. It felt great to get back to the fire and turn around and around to warm my whole body—even though Vicki called me a human hot dog.

Mike started our devotions by reading John 1:9: "The true light that gives light to every man was coming into the world." Mike said that Jesus is our spiritual bonfire. Jesus gives us the light of salvation in our dark world. We feel the warmth of His love when He forgives us and keeps us close to Him.

"Yeah," one of the kids said. "Just like this bonfire doesn't move away from us, Jesus never leaves us either."

"But we sometimes move away from the bonfire," I said, "and then we find out how dark and cold it is."

"That's when it's good to have Christian friends who

can remind you that Jesus' love never goes away," Vicki said. "We can invite people to come close to the fire and feel the warmth."

"That's right," Mike said. "Maybe we can think of my starting the fire as the Holy Spirit planting our faith within us. The fire's heat is like the Holy Spirit's power, calling us through God's Word to believe in Him."

I went home that night, knowing that every time I enjoyed a warm, cozy fire, I'd thank God for giving me Jesus—my spiritual bonfire.

Prayer: Dear heavenly Father, thank You for the warmth of Jesus' love. Keep me close to You and help me lead others to Your Son's light. In His name. Amen.

GOD HELP

Bible Reading: Psalm 18

The sun was trying to warm the earth that cool, fall morning when my brothers Joshua, Daniel, and Aaron and I went down to the river to build a duck blind. As I set a roll of fencing on the river bank, it slid. I grabbed it and sharp wire sliced through my gloves into three of my fingers. By the time my brothers and I got the wire bars cut, my fingers were numb. If I hadn't have been wearing gloves, they would have been cut to the bone.

Looking back on that incident, I'm ashamed to say that I didn't once ask God for help. I tried to do it all myself. How often we respond to life's problems that way.

God is waiting to help us with every problem—a small problem, such as preparing for a test, or a large problem, such as worry over a relative who is in the hospital. In fact, God helps us in every situation, even when we don't ask. Remembering God's presence gives us peace in the middle of worrisome problems.

In Psalm 18, David praises God for delivering him from the hands of his enemies, including King Saul, who was trying to kill him. With David we can say, "The LORD is my rock, my fortress and my deliverer; my God is my rock, in whom I take refuge" (Psalm 18:2).

Martin Luther says that when we begin the Lord's

41

Prayer with the words "Our Father who art in heaven," we are approaching God as children would talk to a loving father. Just as we might ask our dads for something—the use of the car, our allowance, new clothes—we can ask our heavenly Father for what we need. He's listening all the time—while we do our chores, on our way to school, in the midst of problems. He can always help us, even when our earthly dads can't.

I forgot God that day my fingers almost got sliced off. But He didn't forget me. I have a working left hand to prove it.

Prayer: God, help me remember that You are with me at all times, no matter what the problem is, or how big it is. In Jesus' name. Amen.

WHAT KIND OF FISH ARE YOU?

Bible Reading: Ephesians 2:8–10

My brothers and sisters and I gave Dad a fish aquarium last Christmas. After he set it up with gravel, water, and shells, we went to the store with him to pick out some fish. He bought graceful angel fish that glide along slowly, seemingly content to let their food drift to them. He bought quick-moving catfish that constantly suck at the rocks, shells, and sides of the aquarium, eating harmful microorganisms. The angel fish are beautiful to look at, the catfish are hardworking little vacuum cleaners.

Which is more useful—good looks or hard work? What kind of fish are you? Does that sound insulting? Let me change the question. What kind of Christian are you?

In Ephesians, Paul says, "It is by grace you have been saved, through faith—and this not from yourselves, it is the gift of God—not by works, so that no one can boast. For we are God's workmanship, created in Christ Jesus to do good works, which God prepared in advance for us to do" (Ephesians 2:8–10).

First, we are saved by Christ, forgiven and made new through His sacrifice on the cross. Our response to God's grace is the good works He prepares us to do. Our faith shines in our attitude at school, at work, at home, and at church.

Have you seen people called "Sunday Christians"? They may show up at church once in a while, maybe only at Christmas and Easter. Although only God can judge their hearts, we get the idea that they aren't living out their faith through their actions. James 2:17 says, "Faith by itself, if it is not accompanied by action, is dead."

Others can see our faith in our actions—when we help an elderly neighbor with yard work. When we visit a friend who is sick. When we refrain from telling off the person who darts into our parking place.

Christ showed His love for us when He died on the cross to suffer the punishment for our sins. It is Jesus' great act of love that motivates us to serve others.

So, what kind of fish are you? An angel fish that looks pretty and does little? Or a catfish, ready to get to work?

Prayer: God, let me show my faith in You in my life and in my actions. In Jesus' name. Amen.

WINNING

Bible Reading: 1 Corinthians 10:31

I clasped my hands behind my back to hide their shaking. This was nothing like singing at church or school. Bright lights glared in my eyes, hiding the hundreds of people in the auditorium in dark shadows. I could see only the adjudicator, smiling—wickedly I thought—in the first row, his pen poised over his rating form.

I'd made it to the finals in our district music competition. Hundreds of Christian high school kids had spent the day playing instruments, ringing handbells, and singing solos and anthems. Now the winners—who would perform in the closing concert and go on to state competition—were being chosen.

It seemed like every song I'd ever sung flitted through my mind in the seconds before Mrs. Sanders started playing my accompaniment. I remembered sitting next to my mom on the piano bench when I was so little, my feet couldn't touch the floor. "Yes," she had smiled, cupping my face in her hands. "That's just the way to sing. That's lovely." I thought about the happy hours I'd spent in choir, at church and at school. The solos I'd sung at church and in concerts. Everyone always said, "Oh, you look so relaxed and you sing so effortlessly." If they only knew.

Mrs. Sanders smiled and nodded, and played the first notes of "Brother James' Air." I closed my eyes and breathed, "Father, let me forget about myself. Let me sing for You."

"The Lord's my Shepherd, I'll not want ..." Was that my voice, ringing clearly? I forgot the adjudicator and the audience. I sang as I had been taught, thinking about the music, thanking God for answering my prayer.

Afterwards I gathered with the kids from school on the lawn outside the auditorium. We drank Cokes and compared notes on the day. We thought we'd done well with some things and blown others royally. Soon we'd know if any of us would be performing at the concert.

Mrs. Sanders called us back to the auditorium. We sat in hushed silence while our host read the concert performers—the festival winners. Bryan would play his trumpet solo. Christ Central Christian would sing. "First place—female soloist: Claire Brett will sing 'Brother James' Air.' "

I gasped in disbelief, hearing only faintly the cheers of my friends. Somehow I made it backstage and waited my turn to sing. This time I felt elated, yet cool and confident. Singing was a gift God had given me. I would always use it to His glory.

Prayer: Lord, forgive me when I forget You and try to depend on myself. Guide me to use all the talents You have given me to Your glory. In Jesus' name. Amen.

WHEN DEATH ISN'T FAR AWAY

Bible Reading: Romans 8:38–39

Death seemed far away. It was for old people—strangers mostly, or grandparents. Everyone else avoided it too, using words such as "passed away" and "heavenly home." In high school dying is far away.

Then Erin died, and I had to look death straight on. She died. I said it over and over to myself. Only the week before we had been at sports camp together. Then I got the tragic phone call. She had been speeding home along a country road in a storm when she lost control of the car.

I felt betrayed. I had always been the strong, dependable one among my friends. Now I needed help. They seemed ready to be over Erin's death, not willing to listen to my need. I felt used.

Erin died. Suddenly I knew that one day I would die, and that other people I loved would die. I needed something, someone, bigger than me to cope with these thoughts.

God spoke to me in the words of Romans 8. "I am convinced that neither death nor life, neither angels nor demons, neither the present nor the future, nor any powers, neither height nor depth, nor anything else in all creation, will be able to separate us from the love of God that is in Christ Jesus our Lord" (vv. 38–39). That's when I understood that Christ broke the grip of death. Death clung to Him mightily when He hung on the cross. But Jesus rose!

Death could not keep its grip on Jesus, and it cannot keep its grip on us. When we stand at the grave of a loved one in Christ, what looks like defeat is victory. Jesus is victorious over death and, through our Baptism in His name, so are we.

God didn't kill Erin or call out that it was her time to go. Her death was the result of living in a sinful world. But, because of His love for us, Christ conquered sin and death. He gave His life for Erin. And for me. And for you. Nothing will separate us from that love.

> **Prayer:** God, when I lose someone dear to me, I need someone bigger than me to help me cope. Let me put my faith and trust in You. Help me Lord. In Jesus' name. Amen.

POLLUTION

Bible Reading: Psalm 51:7

The industrial revolution brought many changes to our lives and society. New technology makes our lives easier and easier, and there's not too much work left to do without the help of a machine. But the industrial revolution brought changes in nature too.

The beautiful forests God created are being cut down. Water is contaminated and air is polluted. People even have health problems because of pollution.

The industrial revolution, which was supposed to make life better, brought serious problems too. Meetings are held worldwide to address pollution concerns and try to save places that are almost hopelessly polluted.

We do not need to look around the world to find pollution. We can find it in our own hearts. Sin leads us to accept worldly values. To love money and possessions above everything else. To become sexually immoral. To lower our moral standards.

Remaining pure in a polluted world is difficult, but thankfully, a heart filled with God's Holy Spirit leaves little room for pollution. God sent His own Son to die for our selfishness, our polluted morality, our sin. He keeps us close as He calls us to read His Word, to pray to Him, to seek His help. Thanks to Jesus' death and resurrection, purity is possible, even in a polluted world.

Prayer: Thank You for giving me another day in the beautiful world You created. Clean my polluted heart and help me not to obey sinful desires. Let me live for You, through the name of Jesus Christ. Amen.

Elizabeth Horan

Bring Us Together

Bible Reading: Luke 10:25–37

An old man walked tiredly through the park, longing for someone to give him shelter. His hunger drove him to a garbage can, searching for food. He found nothing. He sat on a bench, praying for a miracle, wishing for a Good Samaritan.

The night grew cold, and the old man covered himself with old newspapers. He thought about the tragedies that had led him to this place, with no shelter, no food, no warmth.

His wife and brothers had died. He had no children to care for him and he separated himself from people who might have reached out in friendship. He couldn't understand why God would let these things happen to him. In his desperation, he saw no point in trying to get help.

Suddenly a child's cry startled him. Looking through the bushes behind the bench, the man found a little boy, crying and trying to keep warm with newspapers. The little boy couldn't answer his questions about what was wrong or who his parents were.

Without thinking twice, the old man picked up the little boy and carried him to a shelter. The workers quickly gave the child food and warm clothing. They called the old man a hero, saying the child might have died if he hadn't been found. As the man left, the director asked him his name. "Just call me the Good Samaritan," the old man said as he walked out the door.

In a poem called "Bring Us Together," Marjorie Holmes prays that God would bring together the people who can help each other and enjoy each other. We all have times in our lives, like the old man did, when we long for a Good Samaritan who can be our friend and take care of us. Thankfully, we do have a Good Samaritan—Jesus, who gave His life for us and promises to help us in every need. When we look at His loving example, He points us to those in need and says, "Go and do likewise" (Luke 10:37).

Prayer: Dear Father, bring me together with someone who needs my help. At times when I feel sorry for myself, remind me of the great love You show me in Your Son, and help me to share that love with others. In Jesus' name. Amen.

WHY, GOD?

Bible Reading: Matthew 25:40

"Pelham got shot."

Until my friend told me that, it had been just another cold winter day with nothing to do. I've known Pelham since I was four. He's been like a brother to me, since he and my older brother have always been best friends. Pelham always looked out for me because I was the young one.

We called Pelham the Preacher. We all knew God and loved Him, but Pelham would constantly *do* for the Lord. One day, when Pelham saw an old man cold and shivering with no coat, he gave him his jacket. He didn't even mind giving his jacket away. He said, "The Lord will give back to me."

Pelham's always putting money in the offering at church. And he takes food to people in the neighborhood—even a lady we all know is a prostitute, because he knew she was hungry and didn't have anything to eat.

When I heard that Pelham had been shot, I couldn't help asking God why He let it happen. Pelham never did anything to anyone, except try to be a friend.

Pelham survived. He is out of the hospital and doing the things he used to do. I guess I was wrong to question God's authority when I thought Pelham would die. I know we can't earn God's favor by doing good things. And I know God didn't cause Pelham to get shot. Jesus gave His own life for Pelham and for me, and for all the people in the neighborhood. He says when we help someone else, we are really helping Him. I think that's why Pelham does it.

One day Jesus will thank us for giving Him food when He was hungry and a drink when He was thirsty. He'll say, "I tell you the truth, whatever you did for one of the least of these brothers of Mine, you did for Me" (Matthew 25:40).

That will happen on the last day when Jesus takes us to heaven. I'll be there. I think Pelham will be too.

Prayer: Lord, sometimes I question Your authority. Remind me, even in times of sorrow, that You are ready to help in every situation. Use me to share Your love with everyone who needs my help and Yours. Amen.

Star Talent

Bible Reading: Matthew 25:15

Four seconds left in the game. The Eagles trail by one point. John Hardaway brings the ball down the court. With two seconds left, he lets a half-court shot go. The ball touches the rim and the crowd is silent. It topples into the basket and the crowd screams. The Eagles win by two points and John is declared a hero.

John played a terrific game, as usual. His teammates were happy with their victory, but a little jealous too. Why couldn't someone else be the star, just once? What John's team members didn't always remember was the hours of work John put in to be good, and the sacrifices he made to live up to his potential.

We all feel that type of jealousy from time to time— wanting to do something stupendous without much exertion. Don't you sometimes find yourself thinking, boy, I wish I were the star player? Or, I wish I had a 4.0 and was in the National Honor Society. Or, I wish I were the first trumpet in the band.

Those are the times when you need to realize that God has given you talents and gifts of your own. Some people are good in sports, others are musical, others are academically talented. Some people have a special gift for being good listeners and supportive friends.

You are a shining star in God's eyes. He loves you enough to have sent His own Son to die in your place. In your Baptism you died and rose again with Christ, becoming a new creation.

Time spent wishing to be the star is time wasted. God loves you and blesses you with many gifts. You praise Him when you use your talents to the best of your ability. Pray for the confidence to use your time wisely, develop your talents, and accept yourself as God accepts you. You're a star!

Prayer: Father, keep me strong in my faith and let me learn to be happy with myself. Forgive me when I compare myself to others and feel like I don't measure up. Remind me that I am a true star—Your child. In Jesus' name. Amen.

WHEN GRANDMOTHER DIED

Bible Reading: Romans 8:28

When Grandmother lived with us when I was little, she used to get up early just to brush my long, blonde hair. She was so gentle and kind. But then she got sick.

Grandmother moved back in with us for the last six months of her life. She had become a cranky old lady who couldn't do anything for herself. I tried to be patient with her, but I just couldn't handle it. I began to resent her. I didn't even want to be in the same room with her anymore.

Then she got much worse. I woke up in the morning to find we were taking her to the hospital. We stayed there all day. Grandmother only had hours left to live.

My impatience and resentment haunted me. I had been so cruel to Grandmother. Now what could I do?

Mom and Dad said I could only see her for two minutes. I didn't even know what to say. But Grandmother looked so peaceful. She just looked at me, smiled, and said, "Good-bye. I love you."

That was it. I would never see Grandmother again. The next few months were hard for me. I felt so guilty, I cried myself to sleep every night.

Then one night I asked God to forgive me. I asked Him to give me peace about my grandmother—to be able to feel that she had forgiven me too. I read Romans 8:28 in my Bible, "We know that in all things God works for the good of those who love Him, who have been called according to His purpose."

I felt a great weight lifted off my shoulders. I knew God and my grandmother had forgiven me. I remember Grandmother now as the loving person she was when I was six years old. I miss her, but I know she is in heaven with Jesus. What a comfort!

It's hard to lose someone you love. I wouldn't have made it through my grief over Grandmother's death without my faith in God.

Prayer: Dear God, thank You for being with me in every time of need. When I am troubled and grieving, remind me that You work through all things for my good. In Jesus' name. Amen.

TONGUES OF FIRE

Bible Reading: Romans 12:6–8

Signing autographs after a concert always made me feel a little silly, but I must admit, I loved it. Brian, Kirk, and I had started our Christian rock band, Tongues of Fire, during our junior year in high school. We sang at different churches, parties, and sometimes for relatively big concerts in our area. We were starting to get nice reviews in the local papers, mentioning "fresh rhythms" and "engaging style." None of us were bigheaded enough to think we were on our way to a recording career, but our performing helped us save money for college.

A man's hand stretched out of the gloom into the bright circle cast by the light over the stage door. "Will you autograph my program, please?" I dissolved in laughter. It was Pastor Avanti. He laughed too. "I'd like to talk to you, Jason. Do you have time for a midnight snack?" I said sure, and ran back to the dressing room to tell Bri and Kirk I was leaving.

Pastor and I drove to a Mexican restaurant down the street. We ordered nachos and leaned back to talk. "Jason, you have marvelous musical talent. And when you gave your testimony tonight, it sounded natural and confident. I could sense the Spirit moving through your words, touching people in the audience. The woman next

59

to me was crying. Your words about Jesus' sacrifice on the cross obviously helped her in a very real way."

I sipped my Coke and looked away, embarrassed and not sure what to say. "Jason," Pastor went on, "have you thought about becoming a pastor?" He laughed as I used my napkin to wipe up the Coke that I'd jolted out of the glass when I jumped in shock.

"A pastor? I ... I don't know. No one in my family has ever ..."

Pastor didn't let me finish. "I don't mean to lay a burden on you, Jason. Only a suggestion," he said. "You are gifted in the way you speak and sing. You seem to have an honest desire to tell people the Good News that Jesus is our Savior."

I'd never thought about it before. It had always seemed like the group had just been something fun to do, something that could earn us some money in a fun, sometimes even exciting way. But I did look forward to giving my testimony, to talking with the adults and kids when we sang, and to telling them how much Jesus loved them.

It was a suggestion, Pastor said. Maybe it was a calling. From God Himself. I'd definitely listen.

Prayer: Dear Lord, show me how to serve You in whatever profession I choose. Let me use the skills and talents You have given me to share the Good News that Christ died and rose again with everyone around me. In Jesus' name. Amen.

Elizabeth Winkelman

A RIGHT, OR A MURDER?

Bible Reading: Psalm 139:13–16

The word *euthanasia* comes from two Greek words which literally mean *beautiful death*. Often referred to as "mercy killing," euthanasia means the painless introduction of death to a person for reasons assumed to be merciful.

Supporters of euthanasia have attempted to soften the implications of the act by using such terms as "death with dignity," "assisted suicide," and "choosing the moment." We cannot, however, fool God. He is the Author of life. He has told us, "Do not kill." He alone knows the time for us to be born and the time for us to die. Assisting suicide is, quite simply, murder.

People who support euthanasia differentiate between *active* and *passive* euthanasia. In active euthanasia, people take direct steps to end the lives of persons who are not necessarily dying but who, in their own opinion, feel they would be better off dead. Some people describe active euthanasia as the deliberate easing into death of a patient suffering from a painful and fatal disease.

Passive euthanasia describes situations where a life is taken away by the refusal or the failure to take any kind of medical action or to apply any means of healing. Killing a baby while it is still in the womb is abortion. Leaving a newborn baby to die is called, by some, passive euthanasia. Both are murder. There is nothing beautiful or merciful about an infant's death.

David praises God by saying, "You created my inmost being; You knit me together in my mother's womb. I praise You because I am fearfully and wonderfully made" (Psalm 139:13–14). Our life is precious to God—so precious that He gave up the life of His only Son to win us eternal life with Him. No one has the right to willfully end a life God created.

Prayer: Dear Lord, work in the hearts of those who support euthanasia and other acts of killing. Help them to understand Your ways. Help me witness Your love to people who need to feel Your presence in the midst of pain and suffering. In Jesus' name. Amen.

ARE YOU LIKE YOUR SISTER?

Bible Reading: Leviticus 19:18

My sister got straight As all the way through grade school. She didn't even really have to try. She could study 5 or 10 minutes and ace a test. Through high school she continued to be a straight-A student as well as being in the National Honors Society. She was the yearbook editor and co-valedictorian, with her best friend at her side, achieving the same honor. She was never seen without a thesaurus in her back pocket, and she was a major player in the drama club.

Now in her third year of college, taking 18 credits a semester, my sister is still an absolute overachiever. I, on the other hand, am a normal student who makes average grades and participates in just a few activities which I enjoy.

It's very hard at times to live in the shadow of my sister's reputation for excellence. Every teacher I meet remembers my sister and expects me to perform at her level. Even my parents sometimes expect the same from me, and no matter how I try, I just can't live up to the standard of achievement set by my sister in our family.

As I've grown older I've been able to talk to my parents about the fact that my brother and I don't have the ability to be great students and excel at all kinds of activities as well. It's been hard on all of us, but we are learning that none of us can be a carbon copy of someone else.

God gives each of us special gifts. We have the responsibility to use them to the best of our abilities to glorify Him. Not all of us can be like our neighbors or relatives. But that doesn't mean that we're out of the game plan of life.

God expects from us only what He knows we can do and nothing more. He doesn't call us to be like our neighbors, only to love them. In fact, He tells us to love our neighbors as we love ourselves.

I sometimes envy my sister, but I know God loves me the way I am. He doesn't want me to be like anyone else. He chose me for His child and gave His Son to be my Savior. I'm not exactly like my sister. And that's fine.

Prayer: Lord, help me to understand myself and like myself. Remind me, when I compare myself to others, that You love me the way I am. In Jesus' name. Amen.

OPTIMISTIC? ME?

Bible Reading: Proverbs 17:22

That lost library book will turn up right before it's due! My term paper isn't finished—an act of God will close the school tomorrow!

Optimism. Oh, I know, it's hard to always have a positive outlook on life, and sometimes it isn't even realistic. You probably have so many things going on right now that … But don't stop reading just yet. Being optimistic doesn't have to be that hard!

A message you'll read often in magazines and see on television is, "You can choose to be happy." Not exactly. We can choose to look at the positive rather than the negative, but our deepest happiness comes from the fact that God chose us. Remembering that helps us have a bright outlook and keeps us from dwelling on self-pity. Focusing your attention on other people helps too. Try complimenting someone and see how it makes you feel.

But you say you just went through the most embarrassing situation in your whole life? (*Insert your experience here!*) Try not to be too hard on yourself. We all practice something called self-talk. Saying destructive things to yourself—That was so stupid. Why can't I do anything right?—will just rip you to shreds. When you make a mistake or do something silly, don't respond by saying, "I'm stupid." You're not! Just say, "I made a mistake. Jesus still loves me!" Then examine what happened. Could you have done something differently? Often you'll find it wasn't even your fault! And if it was, you'll know how to handle something similar next time. Lean on God. He'll help you learn from your experiences and keep you close to Him.

Something else to try if you find yourself looking on the down side of things is exercise. Most people feel better after exercising. Friends can also bring up your mood—especially if you hang around others who are optimistic. It's contagious—you'll feel better too. If all else fails, try something new and wild. Take a break from your ordinary routine.

Studies have shown that people with an optimistic outlook on life perform better at school and work, are healthier, and even live longer than people with a negative outlook. God gave you your life as a gift. He sent His own Son to die and rise for you, to win you new life with Him now and eternal life with Him in heaven. That's something to be happy about—something to cheer you up even when you're feeling blue!

Prayer: God, when it's hard for me to have a positive outlook on life, give me Your strength and guidance. Help me remember that You sent Your Son to die for me, and that is happy news, even in the worst of times. In His name. Amen.

GOD'S REST FOR THE WEARY

Bible Reading: Matthew 11:28

"How am I ever going to get everything done?" Sarah groaned. She rolled over on her bed, her mind overflowing with all the things she needed to accomplish that weekend. The stormy weather outside mirrored her dismal spirit. Thunder crashed, matching the pounding in her heart.

Sarah went over the list in her head. Brent had just called. He wanted to do something this weekend. She had to work at her new job Saturday evening, write a four-page report for Social Science (where her work so far this semester had been borderline at best), and learn a solo to sing in church Sunday morning. The fact that she was caught in the middle of a bad fight her best friends were having didn't help. "Ugh!" she moaned.

A knock at the door surprised her. She wiped away a few tears and said, "Come in."

"How are you doing, sweetheart?" Dad said, wrapping his arm around her shoulders.

"I just don't see how I'm going to be able to finish all the things I have to do this weekend, Dad," she said, her tears began to spill again.

"Can I show you something?" Dad asked. He pulled a little card out of his pocket and let Sarah read it. "Come to Me, all you who are weary and burdened, and I will give you rest" (Matthew 11:28).

"I've been carrying this card around since we read the verse in Bible class last week. I've been feeling pretty pressured too. You see," her dad explained, "Jesus knows how it feels to be tired and have too much to do. He experienced a lot of hardships when He lived on earth. He wants you to talk to Him about your problems. He promises to help you with them. Why don't you get some sleep. Tomorrow morning we can talk and figure out some ways for you to get everything done."

"Okay. Good night, Dad." Sarah went to sleep that night feeling much more relaxed. She had learned that talking to God gave her comfort, even in pressured times. Jesus removes the burden of our sin and gives us perfect rest.

Prayer: God, help me trust in You when I have problems. Thank You for letting Jesus carry the burden of my sins to the cross. Thank You for the perfect peace that I'll enjoy in heaven with You forever. Amen.

MY FACE

Bible Reading: 1 Samuel 16:7

I wiped steam off the bathroom mirror and peered gloomily at my face. Naturally, I would develop The Pimple that Ate New York the day that I had to give a report in English. Maybe I could share my insights on the new-frontier theme of American literature with a bag over my head.

Who was I fooling? I didn't care what my face looked like for the speech. But I did care what it looked like afterwards, when I talked to Haley. Would a girl as cute as Haley go out with a guy who had acne like mine? It was a constant, even shameful, embarrassment. The doctor said there wasn't much to do about it. We'd tried some medicine, but it would mainly just take time to clear up. The guys were pretty cool about it. Every once in a while one of them would make a remark about connecting the dots on my face, but usually it didn't come up.

Girls were a different story. Why would a girl want to date a guy with a face like mine? I finished getting ready just as Phil honked outside. Phil was the youth director at my church. He picked a few of us up on Tuesday mornings. We met at McDonald's for a short Bible study, and then Phil drove us to school.

My gloomy mood must have showed because Phil asked what was wrong. I decided to come out straight with it. Phil is pretty good about listening and not preaching. "It's my acne. I want to ask a girl out for this weekend. She's really cute and sweet, and I feel like we'd have a lot in common. But ..." I was too embarrassed to finish.

"You think she won't want to go with a guy who has acne like yours?" Phil asked gently. I nodded. "Brad, this is the truth. When I think about you, even when I see you, I never think about your acne. It's a painful problem for you, I know. But what I think about is your skill in sports, the honest way you deal with your friends, the respect you give your parents. Any girl would be lucky to go out with a guy like you. And she wouldn't think twice about your acne."

"I don't know, Phil," I said. "It's just so noticeable."

"I'm not trying to play down your anguish, Brad," Phil said. "But listen, remember when Samuel went to Jesse's home in Bethlehem to anoint the first king of Israel? God told him not to get excited about how strong and tall Jesse's oldest son was. God said, 'The LORD does not look at the things man looks at. Man looks at the outward appearance, but the LORD looks at the heart' (1 Samuel 16:7). God told Samuel to anoint David, still so young that he had been sent off to tend the sheep."

Phil stopped the car at a red light and turned to me. "Talk to this girl, Brad. Hopefully she'll care about the real you. I think you'll see I'm right."

Something like hope was growing inside of me. Maybe Haley would say yes.

Prayer: God, You judge my heart, not my appearance. Thank You for filling me with faith in Your Son, my Savior. Thank You for washing my sins away. Help me not to judge myself and others based just on physical looks. In Jesus' name. Amen.

RAPE

Bible Reading: Psalm 29:11

The scalding water hissed out of the shower head and burned my body. But no matter how much I scrubbed, I felt like I would never be clean again.

Hot tears poured down my face as the horrible scene of my boyfriend raping me flashed in front of my eyes for what seemed the thousandth time. How could he have done that to me? How could he take something from me that, no matter how much I wanted it, I could never take back? My mind was whirling. Who could I turn to? What should I do? I began to pray. "Please, God, show me what to do."

God made me strong enough to tell my parents. They threw their arms around me in the longest group hug our family ever had. It was the first time I'd seen my dad cry. They got me the help I needed.

Three years later I still feel stabs of pain and betrayal when I look back on that day. The most difficult part is over. There is no more worry—Am I pregnant? Will I get AIDS? Should I tell my parents? What do I do when I see *him* again? What do I say to kids at school?

God answered my prayers that day. He gave me the strength to tell my parents. They helped me get the medical exam and the counseling help I needed. It took a long time to be able to accept myself again without shame, and to trust other people. I had been raped by someone whom I trusted, and whom I thought cared for me.

Looking back, I know God gave me strength that I never would have had on my own. My pastor told me that God sent His Son to die on the cross for me, to suffer in my place. Somehow Jesus felt my shame and anger and pain when He was on the cross. He rose again to win me a perfect, new life with Him. He has washed all my shame and sin away.

I can face things now, without so much fear. I know God will always be with me. He brings me peace in the times I feel afraid.

Prayer: Lord, thank You for giving me the strength to get through the hard times and for promising to stand by me through everything. In Jesus' name. Amen.

TO PROCRASTINATE OR NOT TO PROCRASTINATE

Bible Reading: Matthew 25:1–13

If you are like me, you procrastinate. Whether it's a small assignment or a major project, you probably put it off until the night before, or even later!

I am, in every respect, a typical procrastinator. I even procrastinated on this devotion. Thankfully, there is no way to procrastinate about our salvation. Jesus took care of that.

Let's examine the word *procrastinate*. From the Latin *pro*, meaning *for*, and *cras*, meaning tomorrow, procrastinate literally means "putting off something until tomorrow." The way we often use the word, it means to put something off until a later, indeterminate time.

A textbook example of procrastination is found in the Bible text—the parable of the wise and foolish virgins. Five of the 10 maidens had everything they needed for the upcoming wedding feast. Their lamps were ready, with extra flasks of oil in case the bridegroom should come later than expected. The other five women had their lamps but did not have any extra oil. They made no attempt to get more—until it was too late.

The bridegroom was delayed. When the announcement finally came that he was coming, the five foolish maidens found their lamps nearly out. The five well-prepared virgins had plenty of oil to light the way to the feast.

The foolish women went into the city to buy more oil, but they arrived late. The wedding feast had begun, and the bridegroom denied them admission.

What shall we take away from all this? One thing we never need worry about is being sure we take the time to get saved for eternal life. Our bridegroom—Jesus Christ—took care of that. He died on the cross and rose again to win forgiveness and eternal life for us. Through the faith the Holy Spirit worked in us at our Baptism, we are ready for the bridegroom to come. We are tempted to procrastinate about Jesus' warning to keep watch.

None of us knows when Jesus will return. Matthew 24:36 reads: "No one knows about that day or hour, not even the angels in heaven, nor the Son, but only the Father." By studying the Scriptures, attending worship services, taking the Lord's Supper, and praying to Him, God's Holy Spirit keeps us ready and watchful. Thanks to Jesus, on that last day, we will be welcomed into the great feast instead of being shut out for lack of preparation.

Prayer: Heavenly Father, thank You for the gift of Your Son as our Savior to prepare us for the great feast. Work in us so that we may never procrastinate about our faith or our Christian watchfulness. Bless us as we look forward to the eternal life we will inherit through Jesus Christ, our Lord, in whose name we pray. Amen.

SPRING CLEANING

Bible Reading: Hebrews 9:24–26

When my grandparents were growing up, spring cleaning was an annual event. Once a year, in the spring, the family took all the rugs in the house out into the fresh air and beat the dust out of them that had built up over the long, cold winter. The floors were swept, the furniture dusted, the cobwebs in the corners of rooms wiped away. It was a great feeling to finish the cleaning and walk into a thoroughly cleaned house, rather than a house that had just been cleaned on the surface to look good. Then the family could take the time to enjoy the wonderful spring weather.

In Old Testament times, God instructed His people to have a cleaning day—a Day of Atonement—once a year. On this day the priests made special sacrifices for sin. How good God's people must have felt, knowing that they were cleansed from their sin.

God gave His people the Day of Atonement in preparation for the greatest day of atonement, when Jesus sacrificed His life to atone for the sins of all people forever. Jesus' suffering and death paid the penalty for our sin, and we are no longer separated from God. We are "at one" with Him.

The writer of Hebrews talks about this atonement:

"For Christ did not enter a manmade sanctuary that was only a copy of the true one; He entered heaven itself, now to appear for us in God's presence. Nor did He enter heaven to offer Himself again and again, the way the high priest enters the Most Holy Place every year with blood that is not his own. Then Christ would have had to suffer many times since the creation of the world. But now He has appeared once for all at the end of the ages to do away with sin by the sacrifice of Himself" (Hebrews 9:24–26).

Because of Jesus' death and resurrection, we don't need a once-a-year event to "clean up" our sin. Each day we live in Jesus' forgiveness, washed clean by His sacrifice. What a great feeling it is to be perfectly clean every day!

Prayer: Father, I rejoice that You constantly forgive me for Jesus' sake. Please make me clean from sin this day. Help me love and forgive the people I am with today. In Jesus' name. Amen.

DAVID

Bible Reading: 1 John 3:1

The dance was full of happy people, smiling and laughing. Everyone was having a great time. Everyone, that is, except David.

"Hey, David," I greeted him enthusiastically. Then I realized something was wrong. "Are you okay?"

"Yeah, I'm fine." But he sobbed and turned away in embarrassment. "I'm sorry," he said. "I just don't want to talk about it." And then the problem came out—"It's not my fault that my parents hate each other."

Poor David! I spent the rest of the night talking with him. Coming from a close family, it was difficult for me to understand what he was going through. I began to realize the terrible pain of seeing two people you love so much constantly at each others' throats.

When I got home that night, I began thinking that there was only so much I could do to comfort David. I began to search through my Bible to find a passage that would bring David a message of comfort from God. I decided to share 1 John 3:1 with him: "How great is the love the Father has lavished on us, that we should be called children of God! And that is what we are!"

As David and I talked about this verse, we realized how great it is to have God Himself as our Father. Not only are we heirs of His kingdom, but we receive His protection, comfort, and solace in our troubles. We took David's concerns to God in prayer. We knew God listened and promised to help David.

Because we live in a sinful world, earthly families sometimes experience difficulties and even fall apart. It's painful to listen to parents disagree. It's torture to hear slamming doors and angry words. When you hear it, it may feel like your world is being torn away from you. All your security is vanishing.

Thank God, His family cannot fall apart! When our earthly families have troubles, God calms the waters with His Word and love and forgiveness, shared with us in His family supper.

When your family relationships are troubled, read God's Word and receive His comfort and strength. Pray for healing and solace from the sadness. Talk to your pastor and ask for his advice. God, your Father holds you in the palm of His hand. He forgives the sin of broken relationships and heals the pain of broken homes.

Prayer: Dear Father, heal the brokenness in Your children's homes. Use me to share Your love and comfort with those who need it. Please be with all the Davids of the world, and their families. In Jesus' name. Amen.

THREE IS A CROWD

Bible Reading: 1 John 4:7–12

Cindy and Kelly were inseparable. A casual observer would have trouble telling if Cindy lived at her own house or at Kelly's. They even spent time together doing drills at basketball practice. Then Kelly's grades dropped, and her parents told her she couldn't play basketball anymore until she improved them.

Cindy still went over to Kelly's house every day, but during basketball practice she met a new friend—Cary. Cindy invited Cary to go to Kelly's house with her. They hadn't really noticed Cary before, but now they found they had a lot in common, and soon there were three friends.

After a while Cindy felt that Kelly and Cary were becoming so close that she was being pushed out. It was not fair. After all, she had helped them get to know each other. Cindy confronted Kelly, and Kelly said she understood and was sorry. But things didn't really change. Cindy began to doubt herself. Had she done something wrong, or did Kelly just not like her anymore?

There are many different endings to this story, not all happy, some sad. When we are realistic about relationships, we know that at times we will feel jealous, at times we will be left out, at times we will long for new friends.

In those times it is good to remember the friend who will never leave us, who is never preoccupied with anyone else.

God is always willing to listen to our happy news, and our problems as well. Go to Him in prayer, listen to the advice He gives in His Word, and trust Him to help you work things out. He is always working for your benefit.

Cindy and Kelly grew distant in their relationship. That will happen from time to time with earthly friends, but never with God. He loved you enough to give up the life of His Son for you, and He will always love and care for you.

Prayer: Dear Lord, give me patience and understanding in my relationships with my friends. When things don't go right, guide me and show me Your plans for me. In Jesus' name. Amen.

DEODORANT

Bible Reading: 2 Corinthians 2:15–16

Smells, odor, filth. We all suffer from body odor at one time or another. I'm not talking kiddy sweat; I'm talking grade-A, midsummer, sweat-on-the-back stench. The kind of smell that makes you gag just thinking about it. The aroma that may wash off in two showers, if you're lucky. We've all had it. We are humiliated if we smell that way on a date. Who wants to be with someone who stinks?

Where would we be without deodorant—all the sprays, sticks, and roll-ons—that save us from the embarrassment of smelling like a locker room? No one really ever thinks about deodorant while putting it on, but everyone knows when it's forgotten. Deodorant is designed to reduce, prevent, or cover up unpleasant body odors. That covering up and preventing sounds something like what Christ does with our sins before God our Father.

You might be thinking that comparing Christ to deodorant is silly, but 2 Corinthians 2:15–16 says, "For we are to God the aroma of Christ among those who are being saved and those who are perishing. To the one we are the smell of death; to the other, the fragrance of life."

We are the aroma of Christ. What a great analogy! Have you ever stood outside after a rain in the spring and breathed in the wonderful aroma of God's magnificent creation? What a great feeling to know we carry with us, because of Christ's redeeming work on the cross and the Holy Spirit's empowering, the sweet smells of new life and the forgiveness of sins.

The next time you take a much-needed shower, remember the life-giving work Jesus did for us and the sweet smell of heaven He's won for us.

Prayer: Dear Lord, thank You for giving us the fragrant aroma of forgiven children. Let us be Your aroma in the world, sharing the Good News of salvation in Jesus with all we meet. In His name. Amen.

Power Prayer

Bible Reading: Hebrews 11:1

On October 12 the unthinkable happened. No one could have predicted it. No one could have guessed it. For the first time in our school's history, our cross-country team won the city championship. We won over the favorite and the powerhouse teams. To this day, I firmly believe it was God's answer to prayer that led us to victory.

I remember the day as if it were yesterday. The sky was filled with thick clouds, and thunder rumbled in the distance. Despite the fact that a light rain was falling, our spirited team was psyched to go. Our moods became even more intense as warm-ups progressed and parents and friends arrived. This was no longer just another race; it was *the* race. The race we had spent nearly four months preparing for. The race we wanted desperately to win.

We could feel nervous tension spread throughout the team. Just before the race started, we knelt on the field to pray. Earlier in the day a teammate had sent us all a note with a Bible verse written on it: "Now faith is being sure of what we hope for and certain of what we do not see" (Hebrews 11:1). This would be our focus in the race. The God who helped us in all things would help us run our best.

The gun snapped in the air and the race began.

Towards the middle of the two-and-a-half-mile race, I noticed that our top girl was in first place, leading a field of state-ranked talent. From that moment on, we knew we had a good chance of winning. In cross country, the top five girls' scores count towards the team total, with the lowest scoring team being declared the winner. With five top-25 finishes we were in contention, but it would be close.

Gathered at the finish line, our team was told that we may have won, but it wasn't official yet. In an instant we huddled in prayer—a prayer of thanks to God for allowing us to perform our best, and a prayer of hope for victory.

For what seemed like an eternity the scores were added and re-added. The results were announced. We had won the meet and the city championship by one point!

We felt the sureness of God's presence and strength that day. Never doubt that He will hear your prayers and give you guidance, even in things much more important than city track meets. In times of victory and defeat, sorrow and joy, He remains eternally faithful.

Prayer: Dear Lord, strengthen my faith and give me the guidance of Your Holy Spirit. Thank You for the victory Your Son has already won for me. In His name. Amen.

My Shepherd's Voice

Bible Reading: John 10:2–16

I lay in the tent, too lazy to get up, listening to Kim clank around outside as she started the Coleman stove. It had been a miracle that our parents had let us go camping alone. The trip had been a blast so far.

We set up the tent under cherry and peach trees, full of ripe fruit. A river rushed by the campground, moving so fast that I'd had to grab Sam, my black lab, before he was carried downstream. We'd cooked hamburgers and toasted marshmallows, talking the whole time about our plans for college next year.

"Erin, come out here," Kim poked her head in the tent. Sam squeezed through beside her and landed on my chest. Laughing, I crawled out of the sleeping bag and pulled on my jeans.

"Look," Kim pointed when I came out of the tent. "There's a lamb running along the highway. Do you think we should try and catch it?" Sure enough, a lamb had somehow squeezed through the fence across the road and was running in confusion along the edge of the highway.

"He could get hit by a car," I said. "Let's get him and put him back inside the fence."

It's a good thing the colleges we had chosen didn't have entrance exams on sheepherding. The faster we ran, the faster the lamb ran. Sam, good little herder that he was, ran around the lamb barking crazily, frightening him even more.

We finally collapsed in laughter. At least the lamb was sticking close to the fence and not crossing the highway. Maybe he'd eventually find his way back in. Then a truck came barreling down the road, kicking up clouds of dust. We watched in horror, afraid the lamb would be so frightened that he'd run into the road.

To our amazement, the lamb stopped running and gazed at the truck. A man got out and lifted some sacks of feed from the back of the truck. The lamb ran to him as fast as its legs could go. Far across the field, the flock of sheep started moving towards the truck too.

Kim and I dissolved in laughter again. "It's the shepherd," I said. "The sheep know him!"

That night as we sat looking at the stars, I thought about my Shepherd. That lamb had been afraid to come near us, but he had no fear at all of the truck and the man who cared for him. I'd be leaving home in a few months, traveling to a new school full of strangers. It would be exciting, but frightening too. "Hold me in Your arms, Jesus," I whispered. "I need a Good Shepherd right now."

Prayer: Jesus, Good Shepherd, guide me in the times of my life when I feel frightened and confused about what to do. Keep me safe in Your arms until it is time to live in heaven with You forever. Amen.

THE VICTORY IS WON

Bible Reading: John 16:20

June 17th—a day I'll never forget. I got the bad news that Thursday morning. My teammates and I were dedicated swimmers, and that meant early mornings at the swimming pool, NMW—No Matter What. We were contemplating the icy water and thinking about the sleep we had forfeited. The only thing slightly out of the ordinary was that Pete, who had been with us the night before, was absent from practice.

With or without Pete, practice would continue as usual. It was a hard workout with no time for socializing. Yet without saying a word to anyone, I sensed something was wrong with Pete, and I knew my teammates felt it too.

Halfway through practice Coach called us out of the water. He was blinking back tears as he told us, "Pete was in an accident on Tonkel Road early this morning and … Pete is dead."

Why, Lord? Why did my close friend and teammate have to die? He had so much going for him—varsity member of the Indiana Swim Team and National Team member, and plenty of other honors. Just what happened in this terrible accident? Who was at fault? Surely God wouldn't let something like this happen.

I wrestled with these thoughts for days, until a friend

convinced me to talk to the pastor at his church. I went hesitantly, prepared not to listen, and not to acknowledge a God who could have spared my friend's life.

But I did listen, and to this day, I've never regretted it. The pastor told me that God doesn't want people to die. He sent His very own Son to take our punishment on the cross and rise again to conquer death. He said that God wanted only good for Pete, and for me, and that somehow He would work good, even out of this tragedy. I might never be able to see God's purpose here on earth, but I would understand it clearly in heaven. And, because God had given Pete the gift of faith in His Son, I would see Pete again—in paradise. Everlasting paradise.

Prayer: Dear God, I praise You for conquering death through the death and resurrection of Your only Son. Don't let my earthly concerns get in the way of Your eternal will. Comfort me with the fact that I will be with You in heaven for all eternity. Thanks. Amen.

DON'T LET ANYONE LOOK DOWN ON YOU

Bible Reading: 1 Timothy 4:12

Cockroaches scuttled down the dim hall as I knocked on the door. A child, maybe eight years old, opened the door a crack. She carried a baby wearing only a diaper. I caught a glimpse of smaller children running wildly around the room and a woman, lying in a drunken stupor on the couch. "We're having a show," I told the kids. "Would you like to come?"

Loud music blasting from a speaker filled the neighborhood and attracted children to the run-down camp where we had set up our show. I was on a mission trip with kids from my church, helping share Jesus' love in the South Carolina projects. In this poverty-stricken area, children came willingly when we knocked on their doors, offering free entertainment.

We took turns speaking into a microphone, giving our testimonies about Christ's work in our lives. We performed puppet shows and dramas and dances, all expressing God's love to children who didn't get much love at home.

I held a little girl on my lap and told her about Jesus. She listened intently. I knew she didn't get this kind of attention at home. In her eyes, as I told her that Jesus loved her enough to give His life for her, I was Jesus. I knew I was making a big impact, I pray a saving impact, on this little girl's life.

I realized at that moment that just because I'm young doesn't mean that I don't fit into God's plan or that I have to wait a few years to start serving Him. And I don't have to travel far away on a special mission to start serving Him either. God gives me, and you, plenty of opportunities to serve Him right now. He may help you share His love with a lonely neighbor, a hurting friend, or a family member who needs to know Jesus.

St. Paul told his young helper Timothy, "Don't let anyone look down on you because you are young, but set an example for the believers in speech, in life, in love, in faith and in purity" (1 Timothy 4:12). I remember again that precious little girl that I held in my arms. Maybe the Holy Spirit worked through my words to bring her to faith in Jesus. It didn't matter that I was only a teenager. I was the one who picked up that child that day. Now when I remember her small face, I whisper, "Thank You, God. Thank You."

Prayer: God, please show me opportunities to serve You and others. Help me remember that each day is a gift from You to use in Your service. Thank You for Your never-ending love. In Jesus' name I pray. Amen.

DESIGNER CLOTHES

Bible Reading: Isaiah 61:10

I'm not the kind of person who wastes a lot of money on designer clothes. My parents don't like me to spend *any* money on expensive clothes. They say, when I do buy something that's popular, I'm just spending an extra 20 bucks on some stitching that says the brand name.

But I do like the way I look in designer clothes. I like the way they fit, and I feel that people notice me when I wear them.

The last time Mom went shopping with me, she told me to get an off-brand pair of jeans that were on sale. She said they were a lot cheaper than designer jeans and looked just the same.

I wish I could make my parents understand that it's not just the stitching on designer clothes that make me want to wear them. When I wear name-brand clothes, I think it shows that I care enough about myself to wear clothes that I can take pride in.

A lot of the time I don't feel worth much of anything. That's not easy to say to my parents. I know they don't want me feeling bad about myself all the time. They're just trying to teach me to be careful with my money.

I try to be patient with my parents, but when they pick something out for me that I don't like, we often end up yelling. Sometimes I wish I didn't have such expensive taste in clothes. And I wish that brand names didn't mean so much to me, but they do.

The prophet Isaiah writes, "[God] has clothed me with garments of salvation and arrayed me in a robe of righteousness" (Isaiah 61:10). That means God has clothed me in the love and forgiveness of Jesus. He forgives me for the times when my concern for clothes gets in the way of serving Him and living in His love. I'm asking God to help me talk to my parents and explain how I feel. Maybe we can agree that it's important to have a few nice things to wear.

Prayer: Dear Lord, can You please help me to be more patient with my parents? Help us to be able to talk without yelling. Help me show them that what I wear is important to me. Help me to be proud of myself in the right way—proud of being Your child, not proud of how many possessions I have. You did a good job creating me—let me show that in my actions as well as my looks. In Jesus' name. Amen.

THE RACE

Bible Reading: 2 Timothy 4:7–8

The driver exited the corner, flooring the 450 horse-power V-12 engine. His car shot out, extending the gap ahead of the other racers. He knew the race was his if he could just get around the next corners.

He lined up the car to meet the next corner. He turned the leather-wrapped steering wheel to make a perfect arc. A pothole on the inside angle of the corner sent the car leaping off the track. He fought for control, saving himself from a meeting with the wall, and finally skidded onto the track again.

He kept flying, still widening the distance from the racers behind him. Oil! His car hit the slick at 190 miles per hour, the rear fishtailing. He closed his eyes for the impact that had to come. He waited. He opened his eyes. He was still on course!

He saw the next corner—potholes, oil, water, ice, and things he couldn't even make out, covering the road. Somehow he raced through, and then the brakes squealed, the car stopped, the race was over. He had won.

You are also driving in a race. Your prize is eternal life and your car is the faith God's Holy Spirit gave you in your Baptism. The driver in my story hit a lot of rough spots in the road. There will be a lot of rough spots in your race with God too. You've probably experienced some of them already—sickness; loneliness; the feeling that you don't belong and no one loves you; the death of someone you love; the temptation to be accepted as one of the crowd, even if it means turning your back on your faith; anger and abuse in your family; disappointment when you feel you have failed.

The race driver miraculously sailed over oil and potholes and ice, intact. God is the driver who steers your course. You might not always recognize His guidance and the good things He is working out for you. But you can know He is with you. His Holy Spirit will keep your faith strong. One day your car will finish the race, and you will win. In fact, Jesus has already won the race for you.

Prayer: God, help me through the potholes in my life. Help me to keep believing in You. Thank You for letting Jesus win me the prize of eternal life. Amen.

SEXUALITY

Bible Reading: 1 Corinthians 6:13–20

As he came down the floor, I knew what he was going to do before he did it. It was two-on-one, and he was the ultimate fastbreak passer. He looked through the clear backboard and saw the fans, screaming for a great play. He jumped and pretended to start to shoot, but instead passed the ball behind his back to his trailing teammate who slammed the ball through the basket, giving the final blow to the opposing team.

He'd made that play before, but the crowd loved it anyway. As he left the court, mobs of people gathered around the locker room entrance and chanted his name. He waved and started down the long hallway, lined as usual with beautiful women. He wondered which one he'd spend the night with.

That player had been raised as a Christian. He probably knew the Sixth Commandment—You shall not commit adultery. He probably planned to stop sleeping around one day and marry a nice girl. He probably would not want her to know about his past lifestyle.

When I heard that player had the AIDS virus, it made me sick. I wondered how many other sports players have the virus and are afraid to get tested. I know that God wouldn't send a horrible disease like AIDS to people, but

I think He can use it to help us think twice about our behavior.

God created us as sexual beings. He gave us sex as a gift to enjoy, an intimate gift to share with a husband or wife. He makes it clear that our bodies are not to be used for immoral purposes. Paul writes, "Do you not know that your bodies are members of Christ Himself? Shall I then take the members of Christ and unite them with a prostitute? Never! … Your body is a temple of the Holy Spirit. … You are not your own; you were bought at a price. Therefore honor God with your body" (1 Corinthians 6:15–20).

The threat of AIDS has frightened some popular figures enough that they are rethinking their lifestyles. It probably scares some kids enough to keep them straight too. But fear isn't the motivation that keeps us from sinning in matters of sex. We can honor God with our bodies. God forgives sexual misdeeds as He forgives all sins, through the suffering and death of His Son. We are united with Christ, in death and life. Our bodies are temples for God's Holy Spirit. He will help us use them in ways pleasing to Him.

> **Prayer:** Dear Lord God, help me to enjoy my sexuality in ways that are pleasing to You. Forgive me for the times when I fail, and keep me close to You. In Jesus' name. Amen.

CARE TO TAKE A SPIN?

Bible Reading: Jeremiah 31:34

I remember the first day I got behind the wheel in driver ed. I squinted into the bright sunshine, my hands clammy and my knees weak. I didn't know how I would make my body do what it was supposed to do. I turned the key in the ignition. The engine revved loudly. In my nervousness, I'd pushed my foot down on the accelerator instead of the brake. For the rest of the drive I was so upset about that one single mistake that I had a hard time relaxing and paying attention to traffic. I must confess, I didn't drive well that first day.

Over the next few weeks my driving improved. But that one mistake still haunted me. Each time it was my turn to drive, I'd get really nervous and pray for the drive to be over quickly. I'd been practicing a lot, and without even realizing it, had become a much better driver. But my mistake was always in front of me, blinding me, holding me back from seeing what I had accomplished. My instructor encouraged me, never criticized me, but even that didn't give me confidence.

I kept comparing myself to friends who never seemed to have a problem when they were driving. It became increasingly difficult for me to go to class. The day came to take our final road test. I knew that if I didn't pass this test,

I'd never want to go through it again. I was careful and had a wonderful drive. When my instructor told me that I'd passed with flying colors, I collapsed in relief.

Looking back on that time, I realize that worrying over my mistake kept me from becoming the best driver that I could be. If I would have just concentrated on my driving, instead of lingering on that mistake, I would have enjoyed myself.

It's easy to get into the habit of focusing on a mistake, or something foolish that we did, even on a much bigger scale. We cling to our sin, letting it weigh us down, instead of bringing it before God and asking Him to forgive us.

My driving instructor encouraged me. Because of Jesus' sacrifice on the cross, God is ready and waiting to forgive us and help us live in His love. Jeremiah 31:34 says, "I will forgive their wickedness and will remember their sins no more." That's what God does—He forgives us for Jesus' sake, removing our sins, so that we can live as His children.

If a past mistake is creating a burden in your life, confess it to God now. He is ready to take the weight off your shoulders.

Prayer: Dear God, help me to give You my burdens, and free me from guilt. Help me to know how much You love me. Let me enjoy living in the freedom of being Your child. Thank You, Lord. Amen.

SCARCELY AFRAID

Bible Reading: Psalm 56:3

As I walked through the door my first day of my freshman year in high school, all kinds of questions plagued me. Whom should I talk to? How should I act? Whom should I avoid? What are my teachers like? And the most important question: Am I going to survive this experience?

I was riddled with so many doubts that I thought I would never get through that first day. It was scary to be in a place where I knew hardly anyone. You could smell apprehension in the air. I wasn't the only freshman who was afraid. We had started a journey that would prepare us for college and life.

Then something weird happened. I met people and made friends. I wasn't so apprehensive anymore. I became more at ease with my surroundings and actually began to enjoy myself. I was free to be myself, and made good friends I knew I would treasure forever.

Now I'm a couple of years into high school and loving it. I'm in a Christian school, so I learn about God every day in my theology class. I learn that God is with me always, even at the worst of times. I know He will guide me throughout my life. That doesn't mean that following God is always a bowl of cherries, but it does mean that He loves me and will help me be strong enough to handle what life brings.

How about you? Did you have doubts about your first day at school? Do you feel afraid now? That's okay. We all feel afraid at times. Do what David did. He said, "When I am afraid, I will trust in You" (Psalm 56:3).

Through the gift of His Son, God saved us from the worst fear of all—fear of eternal damnation because of our sin. The God who saved us for eternal life with Him is the same God who is with us in new situations with new people and new challenges. He is cheering us on, leading us through life with Him.

Prayer: Dear Lord, thank You for being with me in the worst of times, when I feel alone and scared. Give me the strength and courage to face new situations, knowing You are at my side. In Jesus' name I pray. Amen.

RELATIONSHIPS

Bible Reading: 1 Corinthians 10:13

"I think it's time to move on in our relationship. I think it's time to have sex," Mike said.

Kelly was startled. "Well, I haven't really thought about it. I mean, I really wanted to wait until I was married."

"Come on, Kelly, nobody waits until they're married these days," Mike said. "You said you wanted us to be closer together, and this will bring us closer together."

"I know I said that," Kelly answered, "but I didn't have sex in mind. I meant talking and really getting to know each other. And I don't want to be pressured to have sex. I want it to be my own decision."

"It will be your decision," Mike said. "But I want you, and I promise I won't hurt you. We can talk tonight."

Kelly thought of nothing else that day. She felt frightened. She knew a relationship must be more than having sex. Her friends who were sexually active said it was great. But maybe having sex with Mike wouldn't bring them closer together. Maybe it would ruin their relationship. And what if she got pregnant or got a disease? And what about all her parents' teaching? God intends sexual intimacy as a gift to save for the person you love more than any other—the person you marry.

Kelly's mind was still racing when she met Mike that night. "Well, have you thought about it?" he asked.

"Yes," Kelly said. "It's the only thing I could think about all day." She took a deep breath. "Mike, I've decided to wait until I'm married, and if you can't respect that, then I think we need to break up."

"No, I understand what you're saying," Mike said slowly. "I get a lot of pressure from the guys to try it. But I should have respected you more."

Sexual intimacy is a constant temptation in relationships, and not all relationships are as healthy and forgiving as Kelly and Mike's. But the God who helps you in all things will help you in relationships too. He says, "No temptation has seized you except what is common to man. And God is faithful; He will not let you be tempted beyond what you can bear. But when you are tempted, He will also provide a way out so that you can stand up under it" (1 Corinthians 10:13).

Prayer: Dear Lord, be with me when I need You most. Make me strong when I am weak and help me to make the right decisions in my relationships. In Jesus' name. Amen.

SUCCESS

Bible Reading: 2 Timothy 4:7–8

For most of us, the need to succeed is an important motivator in everything we try. The satisfaction of success is one of the greatest feelings in the world. Whether it is making a last-second shot to clinch the victory in a basketball game or just reaching a worthwhile goal set years ago, we all dream of success.

Sometimes longing for success may lead to envy. We might envy another person's wealth, strong family, or fame. Envying another's success becomes dangerous when it causes us to hate or feel ill will toward that person.

Many kids are driven to succeed by their own parents. They may feel the only way to gain their parents' love and respect is to be the best in whatever they do or try. Second-best is never good enough for someone caught in this trap. Second-best feels like failure.

A child brought up in a home where success is demanded feels a great amount of pressure. It becomes hard to look at achievement realistically and to realize that failure can be a valuable learning experience.

If you get caught up in the pressure to succeed, remember that Jesus accepts you just as you are, no matter what. He has already won your greatest prize—forgiveness and new life on earth and eternal life with Him in heaven. Talk to your parents, or your pastor or a trusted teacher, about the need to be realistic in your expectations of yourself. Then remember—thanks to Jesus, you have a crown waiting in heaven.

> **Prayer:** Dear Lord Jesus, help me understand the importance of success and failure in my life. Remind me that no matter what I do or say, You will always love me. And only through You will I reach my ultimate success—a place with You in heaven. Amen.

Loss

Bible Reading: Psalm 48:14

In the last four years I lost both my parents. My mom died of breast cancer when I was 13. My dad died last year of bone cancer. I was 16.

I've been through a lot. The hardest thing to bear was seeing what my mom and dad had to go through. I felt like giving up. Sometimes I thought about taking my own life. But then I remembered how much I loved my parents and that I needed to be there for them.

I questioned God—why was He letting this happen? I felt helpless, lost, angry, frustrated, sad. I couldn't think. I wouldn't eat. What would happen to my sister and me? For that matter, what would happen to my parents? I knew about heaven, but when it was right in front of me, I just wasn't sure.

After Mom died and Dad got sick, I really started to question God's power. Why was He doing this? Why was He taking away the two people I loved most?

I never really had a "teenager life." I grew up fast, the "little woman" of the house. After Dad died, I hated life, hated people, and most of all, I hated God.

Because of the total emptiness that surrounded me, I went to see a Christian counselor. He helped me to pray again and to understand that God hadn't killed my parents. God loved my parents and loves me. He took my parents to a home with no pain, the same home that Jesus won for me on the cross. I still question why it had to happen, but I know God will help my sister and me through it.

If you lose someone you love, talk to the people who care for you, and talk to God. He will give you the comfort, strength, and forgiveness that you need. And you don't have to go to God only when you lose someone. You can go to Him when you're sad, alone, in need of help, and even when you're happy and thankful. He always listens.

Prayer: Dear Lord, thank You for always being there for me, especially when I lose someone I love. Help me understand that You are always working for my good, even when loss is hard to bear. In Jesus' name. Amen.

DECISIONS AND PEACE

Bible Reading: Proverbs 3:5–6

"So, Lori, where are you going to college next year?"

"Well, uh …"

"What do you want to study?"

"Well, I'm not sure yet, but …"

"What are you going to do with your life?"

I think almost everyone facing the transition from high school to college, as well as many other new situations and stages in life, feels some apprehension. It seems like everyone asks questions that have no answers.

Worry and apprehension are a result of our sinful human nature. When we feel like our life is in our own hands—we have to decide, we have to plan on our own, we have to handle everything—it is easy to feel overwhelmed. What a lonely and helpless feeling, to face life thinking we have to carry all the weight on our own shoulders.

The good news is that we don't have to face life on our own. The God who has known us since before we were born, and given us salvation through His Son, promises to hold our hand and guide us through every tough decision and challenging situation. We have God's guarantee that He will be at our side, not only when we are traveling on well-worn paths, but also when we can't quite see the path.

We find God's direction for our lives when we read His Word. Proverbs 3:5–6 says: "Trust in the LORD with all your heart and lean not on your own understanding; in all your ways acknowledge Him, and He will make your paths straight."

We can never have all the answers. But God does. When you face a difficult decision or a transition in your life, go to God in prayer. Talk to the people God has given you to care for you about your options. No matter how hard your questions seem, God promises to give you peace in the decisions you make.

Paul's benediction gives us special assurance when we make decisions, "May the Lord of peace Himself give you peace at all times and in every way. The Lord be with … you" (2 Thessalonians 3:16).

Prayer: Dear God, give me guidance and true peace as I make decisions that affect my life. In Jesus' name. Amen.

TAKE THIS JOB AND—
GIVE THANKS FOR IT

Bible Reading: 1 Thessalonians 5:16–18

It was a typical day at work. Long lines. Numerous balloon orders. A women throwing a fit because she was in a hurry. I looked at my watch—two hours to go. I hate this job, I thought to myself. I just want to go home.

If you're like me, you have probably held some sort of a job to save money for college or to earn extra spending money. I started working at a Hallmark shop a year ago to save enough money to buy a car for college next year.

If you've been on a job search, you know that it isn't easy to find one. I was rejected at several places. My self-esteem got pretty low—it seemed as if no one wanted to hire me and I would never find a job. Finally a job opened up and I started to work.

I realized that God had opened a door when I least expected. Even though I know God helped me get my job, I really don't enjoy it, and I wish I didn't have to go to work. A lot of people feel that way about their job from time to time. Jesus certainly understands that experience. He asked God, if it were possible, to let Him turn down the job of going to the cross for our sins. But even in that job, He followed God's will. His suffering earned our salvation.

1 Thessalonians 5:16–18 says something to me about my attitude at work: "Be joyful always; pray continually; give thanks in all circumstances, for this is God's will for you in Christ Jesus."

Does Paul mean that I should really say, "Thank You, God. I love hearing this woman scream at me to hurry. And the way her kid is crying makes me feel very joyful?" I don't think so. But God is giving me the opportunity to earn money, and I thank Him for that.

My job is not forever. I thank God for that too. I'll continue to work, and ask God's help to find another job I can enjoy. I can thank God for the lessons I've learned in this experience too. I've learned that I don't want to be in the retail business as my future career! I've learned how to be a servant to people who need help, and a good steward with my money.

All of my discomfort will be worth it when I have the satisfaction of buying my own car with my hard-earned money. That's something to be joyful about!

Prayer: Dear Lord, help me learn from opportunities that aren't exactly joyful. Help me to be grateful for all that I can learn in the experiences You give me. In Jesus' name. Amen.

VIOLENCE—THE RESULT OF PREJUDICE

Bible Reading: 1 Corinthians 12:12–20

"I see violence and strife in the city. Day and night they prowl about on its walls; malice and abuse are within it. Destructive forces are at work in the city; threats and lies never leave its streets."

That statement could have been made by a newscaster during the 1994 Los Angeles riots, but it wasn't. King David was praying about the unrest and violence in Jerusalem caused by his own son Absalom.

Violence has always been a part of life on earth. The L.A. riots began when four white police officers were acquitted after beating a black man, Rodney King. The city dissolved into chaos: looting, burning, more beatings.

The riots were a result of a disease that our country has always suffered from—prejudice. Sinful people are tempted to hate people of different backgrounds, whether that different background be religious, racial, or a differing lifestyle. Prejudice can be communicated subtly, with a disgusted look, or harshly, with attacks, graffiti, and burning crosses.

Prejudice has no part in God's plan for us. Jesus lived out God's will for His children perfectly. Tax collectors and lepers were considered social outcasts when Jesus lived on earth. Gentiles and Samaritans were discriminated against. But Jesus chose a tax collector as one of His disciples. He healed men with leprosy and associated with Gentiles and Samaritans.

When Jesus asked a Samaritan woman for a drink of water, she wondered why He, a Jew, would even talk to her. Jesus said, "If you knew the gift of God and who it is that asks you for a drink, you would have asked Him and He would have given you living water" (John 4:10). Jesus came to heal differences and forgive sins. He came to suffer and die for all people, of all races and backgrounds, to win them eternal salvation.

No matter our color or background, we become God's children when we are baptized. Paul tells us, "For we were all baptized by one Spirit into one body—whether Jews or Greeks, slave or free—and we were all given the one Spirit to drink" (1 Corinthians 12:13). He goes on to explain we are all part of the body of Christ—each part as important and necessary as the next.

Prejudice comes from ignorance. We tend to fear or hate what we do not understand. Jesus' example calls us to learn about each other's differences and accept them.

Prayer: Dear Lord, help me to admit and overcome my ignorance and feelings of prejudice. Thank You for making each person special, with unique gifts and talents. Help me work together with people of all races and backgrounds to further Your kingdom. In Jesus' name. Amen.

Shana Opdyke

THERE IS NO "I" IN T-E-A-M

Bible Reading: 1 Corinthians 12:21–31

You look up at the scoreboard and see that there are only 15 seconds left. The score is 68 to 67. Your team is losing by one point. Your coach calls a time-out. Quickly, she draws a new play on her white scratchboard. She tells you how to run the play and reminds you how important this championship game is—as if you could forget. You walk back on the court, knowing that every player must do her job perfectly for one person to score.

Basketball is a highly competitive sport. I admit that no one will ever be tempted to call me a female Michael Jordan, but I can hold my own on the team. Last season, I began to get depressed about the way I was playing. I was trying my hardest to score, but I wasn't getting many points. The team was winning, but I didn't feel I was contributing. One night, after a great win, I cried on the bus ride home, feeling like the smallest and worst player on the team.

The next day I talked to my coach. She helped me to see that every player is important. The girl who sits on the bench most of the game, cheering the team to victory, is as important as the player who scores 25 points. She said, "There is no 'I' in team."

My coach's words reminded me of what God says in

114

His Word, "If one part suffers, every part suffers with it; if one part is honored, every part rejoices with it" (1 Corinthians 12:26). In feeling bad about my own playing, I could have lowered the spirits of the whole team. Playing with an all-for-one-and-one-for-all attitude gave the team extra spirit and energy.

Never feel that you aren't as talented or useful as someone else. God chose you to be His child in Baptism. He gave the life of His only Son to win you forgiveness and a place with Him in heaven. He uses you, with the gifts and talents He gave you, as a part of His team.

In 1 Corinthians 12, God is talking about Christ's body, the church. As Christians, we work together to share God's love with one another and with all who need to hear it. You might have the talent to sing well or be a great athlete. You might have the gift of teaching, or of helping people build friendships. Whatever gifts you have come from the Lord. Never feel that you are an unimportant or unneeded member of His team. God uses your skills, in ways you may not even always understand, to bring the Good News of what He has done in Jesus to all who need to hear it.

> **Prayer:** Dear Lord, I know that I am not the best at everything I do. Help me to use my gifts and talents with others to show Your glory. In Jesus' name. Amen.

FAITH LIKE A CHILD

Bible Reading: Mark 10:14–15

A few of years ago my two sisters and I spent the night with some friends while my parents were out of town. As we were getting into bed, I looked at my sisters. Amanda hugged the special pillow that she couldn't sleep without. I glanced at my own arms, tight around my ever-necessary teddy bear. Then I looked at my four-year-old sister Katie, and my mouth dropped open.

Katie was holding a picture of Jesus! "Why did you bring that?" I asked.

"Because I can't sleep without it," she answered.

When the disciples tried to tell the mothers bringing their little children to Jesus to get lost, Jesus held up the children's faith as an example. He said, "Let the little children come to Me, and do not hinder them, for the kingdom of God belongs to such as these. I tell you the truth, anyone who will not receive the kingdom of God like a little child will never enter it" (Mark 10:14–15).

Remember, how when you were little, you believed everything your parents told you? My dad said if I put my arm out of our car when it was moving, it would blow off. My dad would never have been able to prove that to me, but he didn't have to. I believed him. That's the kind of faith Jesus is talking about—faith that believes without requiring proof.

As we get older, we tend to question things. We start to wonder who Jesus really is, and if He really did all the things described in the Bible. We begin to doubt God's ability to help us in every situation. We begin to doubt our own value in His world.

In those times, we ask God's Holy Spirit to give us the faith of a child. A child believes without requesting explanations. A child begs for more. Once we hear about Jesus' love, we long to hear all about what He has done for us, and how we can live according to His will.

In times of questioning and doubt, remember Katie, who took Jesus to bed with her. There was no doubt in her mind. Jesus would stay with her and give her a good night's sleep. Jesus is with you too. He forgives your doubting and gives you the trusting faith you need to accept Him as your Savior and Friend.

Prayer: Dear Jesus, help me remember what it's like to be a little kid. Give me unconditional faith in You and the desire to learn more. In Your name I pray. Amen.

MOTIVATION

Bible Reading: Colossians 3:23–24

The minutes slowly ticked by as George stared blankly at the intimidating algebra problems. Why, why didn't I study last night? he thought. This test is worth 20% of my algebra grade, and I just blew it off. If I would have spent as much time studying as I did watching the football game, I would have been able to get a decent grade.

George had that conversation with himself often. He'd had plenty of time to study the night before but, as usual, found plenty of excuses not to. First he watched television. Then he played some basketball. Then he went to Steve's house to watch the football game. Then he needed a snack …

The bell rang, breaking George's train of thought. It took him a moment to realize class was over. Shaking his head in disgust, he turned in his half-completed test.

When George went home that evening, he sulked about his failing grade. He blamed his teacher for making the test too hard. He blamed just about everybody and everything except himself.

We all act like George from time to time. As busy as we are, it's easy not to finish homework, do assignments carelessly, spend too little time studying, and not work our hardest. But when we fail to work to our full potential, we are cheating ourselves and not living up to the abilities God has given us.

God tells us, "Whatever you do, work at it with all your heart, as working for the Lord, not for men, since you know that you will receive an inheritance from the Lord as a reward. It is the Lord Christ you are serving" (Colossians 3:23–24). Whether we are studying or playing football or watching a little brother, God challenges us to do our best. His own Son didn't work halfheartedly for our salvation. Jesus experienced every temptation and sorrow we can know, was deserted by His friends, suffered agony and death in our place. His death and resurrection won us forgiveness for the times we try just hard enough to get by.

When you find yourself thinking like George, ask Jesus for help. He will remind you, "I can do everything through Him who gives me strength" (Philippians 4:13).

Prayer: Dear heavenly Father, help me to do my best in my schoolwork and all my tasks, even when there are other things I'd rather be doing. Remind me that I glorify You when I use the gifts You have given me fully. In Jesus' name. Amen.

SHOPLIFTING

Bible Reading: 1 Corinthians 15:33–34

Judy and I went with the rest of the basketball team to the mall. We'd played a great game, and now it was time to relax. We packed together for Cokes and hot dogs and discussed our plays. Then Jackie, our captain, decided she wanted to shop.

We followed Jackie into a music store. Brenda and Judy kept a lookout for security guards and clerks while Jackie stuffed her jacket pockets with cassette tapes.

I stood frozen, breathless. This was wrong. But I did not walk away. I followed them to the next store. I was the new kid on the team. They were the popular kids, on the team and at school. I wanted them to like me.

In the Hallmark store, Judy asked me if I wanted anything. I saw a cute book for telephone numbers and asked her to get it. Judy stuck it in her pocket, and we walked casually out of the store.

We still aren't sure what happened, but somebody must have seen us and called the principal at our school. He was very disappointed in me for taking part in something so foolish. He told me that I had let him down even more than the others because he expected more from me. He suspended us all.

I spent that day at home thinking about what I had

done. I knew all along that it was wrong, but I was so caught up in wanting to fit in that I shut God out of my mind. My parents said I shouldn't let wanting people to like me have so much power over me. My dad read a verse from the Bible, "Do not be misled: 'Bad company corrupts good character.' Come back to your senses as you ought, and stop sinning; for there are some who are ignorant of God" (1 Corinthians 15:33–34).

I confessed what I had done to God and asked His forgiveness. I asked Him to make me strong enough to be my own person. Unless Judy and Jackie and Brenda and the rest are willing to change, I won't be able to associate with them. God has a plan for my life, and I don't want so-called friends to lead me off on the wrong track.

> **Prayer:** Lord, help me live as Your child. Forgive me when I follow the ways of friends who go against Your will. Mold me into the person You want me to be. In Jesus' name. Amen.

GRANDMA'S FAITH

Bible Reading: Hebrews 12:1–3

I had a sudden craving for Malt-O-Meal. Mom picked some up for me at the store.

"I don't know how you can stand that stuff," Mom said when she brought it home. Actually, I didn't know either because I hadn't eaten it in years. But a craving is a craving, and I just had to have some.

Why am I fixing this? I wondered as I turned on the microwave. It's nine o'clock at night, and I want hot cereal? As I opened the door and reached in to stir the cereal, the aroma drifted out. I suddenly realized why I wanted it so much, and tears came to my eyes. I was overwhelmed with the memory of my grandma, who had died the year before. Whenever I was sick and stayed at her house, she fixed me hot cereal. Now on the anniversary of her death, that memory came back to me.

It's comforting to know where Grandma is now. Her death has somehow made eternal life a reality for me. Someone I love is seeing Jesus face-to-face every day! Grandma is proof of the salvation Jesus won for you and me.

If only I could tell Grandma how much her faith in Christ Jesus affected me and how I carry it with me every day. She told me about the miracles God had worked in our family, and how I was one of them, just for being born. She told me to hold fast to God during struggles, and He would make my faith strong.

The writer of Hebrews says, "Since we are surrounded by such a great cloud of witnesses, let us throw off everything that hinders and the sin that so easily entangles, and let us run with perseverance the race marked out for us. Let us fix our eyes on Jesus, the author and perfecter of our faith" (Hebrews 12:1–2). Grandma is in my cloud of witnesses. She is cheering me on as God gives me the strength and faith for what lies ahead.

I want to keep God first throughout my life, just as Grandma did. I want to raise my children and my grandchildren with as much love and faithfulness to Christ as she had. I know these things will happen because Grandma isn't my only example. Jesus is the author and perfecter of my faith. He died and rose again to win me forgiveness and new life. God's Holy Spirit gave me faith in Him through my Baptism.

By stirring some Malt-O-Meal, God allowed me to hear and see and feel an experience from many years ago. It was almost like Grandma was there, telling me, "Don't forget. I'm still very much alive—not just in your memory but in the Father's kingdom!" Thank you, Grandma, for being such a wonderful witness. I will never forget.

Prayer: Dear Father, give me the confidence to be a bold witness of Your Gospel. Let Your love shine in me and inspire the faith of others until I meet You in heaven. In Jesus' name. Amen.

STUCK IN THE MUD?

Bible Reading: Romans 5:1–5

One night, a little over a year ago, our family station wagon got stuck in the mud after I had parked it in the grass next to our driveway. I didn't think much about it and took my mom's car to the field for soccer practice. But when I got back at 9:30 that night, I realized that we would need both cars in the morning so my parents could go to work and my brother and I could go to school.

It was well past midnight when my brother and I finally extricated the mammoth vehicle from the mire. We had tried everything—most of our efforts causing the car to sink ever deeper into the mud. When we miraculously hit upon the proper solution, I felt the contentment of persevering through adversity. Covered with mud from head to toe, my back aching and eyelids drooping, I thought about the many different ways we can get "stuck in the mud" in our lives.

We all experience setbacks, breakups, and disappointments. We may fail an important test, fail to make a team or fail to impress the crowd with our playing, break up with someone who means everything to us, or lose someone we love to illness or death. Paul tells us, "We also rejoice in our sufferings, because we know that suffering produces perseverance; perseverance, character;

and character, hope. And hope does not disappoint us, because God has poured out His love into our hearts by the Holy Spirit, whom He has given us" (Romans 5:3–5).

God works through the obstacles in our school life, social life, and spiritual life to make us strong and keep our eyes focused on Him. He sent His Son to earth to overcome every muddy problem we might face. We rejoice in the glory Jesus won for us, and in the sufferings we experience as we follow Him now. Jesus won the hope of heaven for us. That hope will not disappoint us because it is a gift of God's love given to us by His Holy Spirit.

Prayer: Dear God, give me the strength to persevere through life's hardships. Help me to know that You are with me always, and will be there when I need You most. In Jesus' name. Amen.

CELEBRATION

Bible Reading: 1 Corinthians 15:56–57

I grabbed Nate's arm before he could send his bulletin-airplane sailing over the balcony rail. Glancing down, I saw Pastor Jeff staring in horror under the pews. Kiesha and Darrel were crawling through peoples' legs up to the altar where the kids from our youth group were presenting the Good Friday chancel drama we had written.

Good Friday? Black Friday. Our week as Servants for Christ at the central-city Cincinnati church had been thrilling up until now. Six of us had traveled together from our church in Nebraska. Pastor Jeff had greeted us with the words, "You can help me plan the greatest Easter celebration we've ever had."

Hank, the church janitor, had moved out of his room in the parish hall so Lacey, Liz, and I could stay there. Pastor Jeff pointed out that the room had been rat-proofed—the holes in the walls had been filled with plaster. Tim, Chad, and A. J. were staying with members of the church down the street.

The week flew by. Hank took us to an Alcoholics Anonymous meeting. He stood up and said that he had spent time in jail for theft and had lived in an alcoholic stupor until Pastor Jeff had talked to him about Jesus. Now he worked at the church and hadn't had a drink in six months.

He praised God for the new life God had given him.

We went with Pastor Jeff to make calls. We learned to yell before we went down an alley, sending all the rats scurrying to hiding places. We entered dark, dilapidated apartment buildings with overflowing trash cans sitting in the hallways. Pastor invited everyone to come to the church and get to know us, and to be sure and come to our Easter celebration.

We invited every kid we saw to come over to the church every evening for games, music, and stories about Jesus. By Wednesday night we had 75 children thrilled at the thought of singing as a choir on Good Friday and Easter. Lacey and Tim and I presented puppet shows about Jesus, while Liz and A. J. and Chad played pool with the older kids and led Bible study. Over and over we told the kids, Jesus loves you. He loves you so much, He gave His life for you. Then He rose again so that you can live with Him in heaven.

Good Friday. Our week exploded in disaster. Pastor Jeff was so disappointed in the kids' behavior in church that he left without talking to us. That night we heard a gun shot in the street. In the morning Chad told us that one of the kids who had been coming to Bible study had been shot. He might not live. Pastor Jeff came and told us about Hank. He had been arrested, drunk.

Easter morning dawned and we gathered early in the church. We felt no excitement, only relief that the week was over. Then the kids started arriving, faces shining and many of them wearing new clothes. Their families filled the church. The kids sat like angels, then stood to belt out "Jesus Christ Is Risen Today." We couldn't stop grinning. God did work miracles, and the greatest one was raising His Son from the dead for us, and for these kids.

Pastor Jeff had tears in his eyes as we climbed into our van to start home. "We did it," he said. "We had our Easter celebration."

Prayer: Jesus, let me shine with Your love wherever I am. When it seems like I'm failing, remind me that it is You who works through me to accomplish Your will. Amen.